THE
TRUTH
of
GOD

THE

TRUTH

of

GOD

GREGORY A. BROWN

XULON PRESS

Xulon Press
2301 Lucien Way #415
Maitland, FL 32751
407.339.4217
www.xulonpress.com

Xulon PRESS

Unless otherwise indicated, Scripture quotations taken from the New King James Version (NKJV). Copyright © 1982 by Thomas Nelson, Inc. Used by permission. All rights reserved.

Scripture quotations taken from the New American Standard Bible (NASB). Copyright © 1960, 1962, 1963, 1968, 1971, 1972, 1973, 1975, 1977, 1995 by The Lockman Foundation. Used by permission. All rights reserved.

Printed in the United States of America.

ISBN-13: 978-1-5456-7404-8

First of all, I would like to dedicate this book to my wife, Lynnette (Sandi), whose faith is beyond compare. A big part of my dedication is to the Bible. I have read it through several times, but need to read it through many, many more times. I have learned that not only reading the Bible, but also discussing the Bible with others helps my understanding. The more that I read and discuss The Bible, the more I learn. I would also like to dedicate this book to the members of my small church. All of them help me with my growing understanding of God's Word. And I would like to dedicate this book to my family in the Philippines and to my family here in America.

CHAPTERS

~

PREFACE

∞

This book is about my search for religious truth. The Bible is Truth, but which interpretations of the Bible that we are taught are true and what interpretations are false or misleading?

Most of the Bible was written over 2,000 years ago. Many new teachings, in the form of interpretation, have been added well after 95 AD, after John wrote Revelations on the island of Patmos. These additions and false teachings were wrong then and they are wrong now, but they have been accepted as truth because they have been repeated over and over again. My goal has been to seek God and only follow the Truth.

Who am I?

I grew up in the 60's as a Methodist. I attended church regularly with my parents. I played guitar with the youth group at church. I spent several weeks each summer, in Illinois, with my grandparents and attended their church. They went to the Christian Pentecostal churches. The kind of church where the Spirit was moving in full force with shouting and jumping and people speaking in tongues. Then, when I was in High School, I started to grow away from the church. My parents were killed by a drunken teenager in a head-on collision in 1975 and that sent me into a tailspin for the next 20 years. I turned to alcohol and was on a destructive life course. I married several times and could never find true happiness.

In 1995, I picked up the Bible and read it through. I started attending church again. I was baptized into Christ. By '97, I had read the Bible through about three times and became interested in prophecy. I was also discovering some teachings of mainstream churches that just did not agree with the teachings of the Bible. The big problem that I discovered was that we were worshiping on the wrong day. Why and when was the Sabbath changed to Sunday? Why were we celebrating the birth of Jesus on the wrong day? Why and when did the church eliminate the Holy Days given to us by God and replaced them with holidays that were given to us by pagans? I had lots of questions and no good answers. I would ask preachers and leaders in the church and was told the standard (wrong) answers – that The Sabbath has been changed to the first day of the week, that the Christians have replaced the Jews, that the Holy Days were only for the Jews and not the Christians, and several more. My first thought was that it just didn't make any sense. Jesus is our savior and Jesus was a Jew. In fact, the whole Bible was written by Jews except for the book of Luke. The Bible says it and I have always been taught that God does not change. (**Malachi 3:6**- For I am the LORD, I change not; **Hebrews 13:8**- Jesus Christ is the same yesterday and today and forever.) So who changed what and when did they do it?

My first concern was "why was the 7th day changed to the first day" – from the Sabbath to Sunday? Then, I discovered the origins of Christmas and Easter. The more that I learned, the more questions I had. God was the God of "Truth" not of lies. The way that I look at it, if something is based on a lie, no matter how any "truths" you may add to it, it is still a lie. "Faith" is the most important relationship that I have with God and for me to have "Faith", I need to believe in the Truth.

It is this search for the "Truth" that has led me to write this book. The Bible, both the Old and the New Testaments are "Truth". It is the misunderstanding of scripture and the additions to God's Word that has caused me the problem. I have always wondered why anyone would add to or change the Bible, when the warning is very clear –

Revelation 22:18, 19–I warn everyone who hears the words of the prophecy of this book: if anyone adds to them, God will add to that person the plagues described in this book; if anyone takes away from the words of the book of this prophecy, God will take away that person's share in the tree of life and in the holy city, which are described in this book.

Proverbs 30:2-6, surely I am too stupid to be a man. I have not the understanding of a man. I have not learned wisdom, nor have I knowledge of the Holy One.

Who has ascended to heaven and come down?
Who has gathered the wind in his fists?
Who has wrapped up the waters in a garment?
Who has established all the ends of the earth?
What is his name, and what is his son's name?
Surely you know! Every word of God proves true;
he is a shield to those who take refuge in him. Do not add to his words,
lest he rebuke you, and you be found a liar.

Deuteronomy 4:2–In your observance of the commandments of the LORD, your God, which I enjoin upon you, you shall not add to what I command you nor subtract from it.

My goal with this book is only to seek and point out the truth, not to point blame or find fault. I do not make any claim on knowing more about the Bible than the next man. I just want to share the knowledge that I have. I would like to spark your interest in learning more.

I am only a talmadin, a disciple, a student passing along the little knowledge that I have learned – so far….and that I am still learning.

Chapter 1

MY SEARCH FOR TRUTH
IN RELIGION

∞

My search began when I realized that Christmas was wrong. Jesus was not born in the winter. He was born in September/October. This can be traced back using the Bible and the Holy Days (Feasts) and when shepherds were in the fields. The time of Christmas was changed to the time of the winter solstice. It reflects the birth of the sun, not the birth of the Son. There is only one festival at that time of year that is biblical and that is the Feast of Lights. The Feast of Dedication, or Hanukkah, is a Jewish holiday also known as the Festival of Lights. Hanukkah is celebrated during the Hebrew month of Kislev (November or December), beginning on day 25 of Kislev and continuing for 8 days. The story of Hanukkah is recorded in the Book of Maccabees, which is part of the Apocrypha. The Feast of Dedication is mentioned in the New Testament **John 10:22-23**. [22] At that time the Feast of the Dedication took place at Jerusalem; [23] it was winter, and Jesus was walking in the temple in the portico of Solomon.

Prior to the year 165 BC, the Jewish people in Judea were living under the rule of the Greek kings of Damascus. During this time

Seleucid King Antiochus Epiphanes, the Greco-Syrian king, took control of the Temple in Jerusalem and forced the Jewish people to abandon their worship of God, their holy customs, and reading of the Torah. He made them bow down to the Greek gods. According to ancient records, this King Antiochus IV defiled the Temple by sacrificing a pig on the altar and spilling its blood on the holy scrolls of Scripture. As a result of severe persecution and pagan oppression, a group of four Jewish brothers led by Judah Maccabee, decided to raise up an army of religious freedom fighters. These men of fierce faith and loyalty to God became known as the Maccabees. The small band of warriors fought for three years with "strength from heaven" until achieving a miraculous victory and deliverance from Greco-Syrian control..

After regaining the Temple, it was cleansed by the Maccabees, cleared of all Greek idolatry, and readied for rededicated. The rededication of the Temple to the Lord took place in the year 165 BC, on the 25th day of the Hebrew month called Kislev.

Hanukkah is called the Feast of Dedication because it celebrates the Maccabees' victory over Greek oppression and the rededication of the Temple. But Hanukkah is also known as the Festival of Lights, and this is because immediately following the miraculous deliverance, God provided another miracle of provision.

In the Temple, the eternal flame of God was to stay lit at all times as a symbol of God's presence. But according to tradition, at the time that the Temple was rededicated, there was only enough oil left to burn the flame for one day. The rest of the oil had been defiled by the Greeks during their invasion, and it would take a week for new oil to be processed and purified. However, at the rededication, the Maccabees went ahead and set fire to the eternal flame with the remaining supply of oil. Miraculously, God's Holy presence caused the flame to burn for eight days until the new sacred oil was ready for use.

The other holiday that is wrong is easter. This should actually be the Holy Day of Passover. Passover is not celebrated with sexual fertility symbols–eggs, rabbits, etc. Follow the Hebrew calendar for the correct day. Passover was when the Jews used the blood of a lamb and put it on their door frame (Hebrew letter chet) so that evil would pass over their family. **Exodus 12:21-28** [21] Then Moses called for all the elders of Israel and said to them, "Go and take for yourselves lambs according to your families, and slay the Passover *lamb*. [22] You shall take a bunch of hyssop and dip it in the blood which is in the basin, and apply some of the blood that is in the basin to the lintel and the two doorposts; and none of you shall go outside the door of his house until morning.

[23] For the LORD will pass through to smite the Egyptians; and when He sees the blood on the lintel and on the two doorposts, the LORD will pass over the door and will not allow the destroyer to come in to your houses to smite *you*. [24] And you shall observe this event as an ordinance for you and your children forever. [25] When you enter the land which the LORD will give you, as He has promised, you shall observe this rite. [26] And when your children say to you, 'What does this rite mean to you?' [27] you shall say, 'It is a Passover sacrifice to the LORD who passed over the houses of the sons of Israel in Egypt when He smote the Egyptians, but spared our homes.'" And the people bowed low and worshiped.

[28] Then the sons of Israel went and did *so*; just as the LORD had commanded Moses and Aaron, so they did.

The Hebrew letter "chet" looks like a door frame. The Hebrew people were instructed to use the blood of the sacrificial lamb and paint the doorframe so that the LORD would pass over the door and not allow the destroyer to come in. The significance of the CHET is affirmed in the expression chayeh chaim (Life of Life), meaning God. This refers to the highest of the three levels of loving God, where the Divine Presence is fully revealed. This occurs once one is fully aware that every form of life and lifelessness depends upon the Life of Life.

Learning these things, I looked into the 10 commandments. The 4th commandment is the Sabbath–Saturday! **Exodus 20:8-11**

"Remember the Sabbath day, to keep it holy. Six days you shall labor and do all your work, but the seventh day is a Sabbath of the LORD your God; *in it* you shall not do any work, you or your son or your daughter, your male or your female servant or your cattle or your sojourner who stays with you. For in six days the LORD made the heavens and the earth, the sea and all that is in them, and rested on the seventh day; therefore the LORD blessed the Sabbath day and made it holy.

Revelation 14:12

Here is the perseverance of the saints who keep the commandments of God and their faith in Jesus.

Chapter 2

THE BIRTH OF JESUS

∞

T he best way to determine the time of Jesus' birth is to use the timing of the Holy Feasts, which the Jews kept accurate account of. To find out when Jesus was born, we need to go back and use the Hebrew calendar, find out the conception of John the Baptist, and look at the Jewish feasts.

The Jewish calendar begins in the spring, during the month of Nisan (Esther 3:7 *In the first month, which is the month Nisan, in the twelfth year of King Ahasuerus, Pur, that is the lot, was cast before Haman from day to day and from month to month, until the twelfth month, that is the month Adar*.), so

the first "course" of priests, would be that of the family of Jehoiarib, who would serve for the first week of Nisan, Sabbath to Sabbath.

The second week would then be the responsibility of the family of Jedaiah.

The third week would be the feast of Unleavened Bread, and all priests would be present for service.

Then the schedule would resume with the third course of priests, the family of Harim.

By this plan, when the 24th course was completed, the general cycle of courses would repeat. This schedule would cover 51 weeks or 357 days, enough for the lunar Jewish calendar (about 354 days). So, in a period of a year, each group of priests would serve in the Temple twice on their scheduled course, in addition to the 3 major festivals, for a total of about five weeks of duty.

To pin point when Jesus was born, we first need to find out when John the Baptist was born. First, to find out when **John the Baptist** was conceived we need to start with Zacharias, the father of John the Baptist.

Luke 1:5-24—Birth of John the Baptist Foretold

[5] In the days of Herod, king of Judea, there was a priest named Zacharias, of the division of Abijah; and he had a wife from the daughters of Aaron, and her name was Elizabeth. [6] They were both righteous in the sight of God, walking blamelessly in all the commandments and requirements of the Lord. [7] But they had no child, because Elizabeth was barren, and they were both advanced in years.

[8] Now it happened *that* while he was performing his priestly service before God in the *appointed* order of his division, [9] according to the custom of the priestly office, he was chosen by lot to enter the temple of the Lord and burn incense. [10] And the whole multitude of the people were in prayer outside at the hour of the incense offering. [11] And an angel of the Lord appeared to him, standing to the right of the altar of incense. [12] Zacharias was troubled when he saw *the angel*, and fear gripped him. [13] But the angel said to him, "Do not be afraid, Zacharias, for your petition has been heard, and

your wife Elizabeth will bear you a son, and you will give him the name John. [14] You will have joy and gladness, and many will rejoice at his birth. [15] For he will be great in the sight of the Lord; and he will drink no wine or liquor, and he will be filled with the Holy Spirit while yet in his mother's womb. [16] And he will turn many of the sons of Israel back to the Lord their God. [17] It is he who will go *as a forerunner* before Him in the spirit and power of Elijah, TO TURN THE HEARTS OF THE FATHERS BACK TO THE CHILDREN, and the disobedient to the attitude of the righteous, so as to make ready a people prepared for the Lord."

[18] Zacharias said to the angel, "How will I know this *for certain*? For I am an old man and my wife is advanced in years." [19] The angel answered and said to him, "I am Gabriel, who stands in the presence of God, and I have been sent to speak to you and to bring you this good news. [20] And behold, you shall be silent and unable to speak until the day when these things take place, because you did not believe my words, which will be fulfilled in their proper time."

[21] The people were waiting for Zacharias, and were wondering at his delay in the temple. [22] But when he came out, he was unable to speak to them; and they realized that he had seen a vision in the temple; and he kept making signs to them, and remained mute. [23] When the days of his priestly service were ended, he went back home.

[24] After these days Elizabeth his wife became pregnant, and she kept herself in seclusion for five months,

With this information from Luke, we can find the time when John the Baptist was conceived.

Beginning with the first month, Nisan, in the spring (March-April), the schedule of the priest's courses would result with Zacharias serving during the 10th week of the year. This is because he was a member of the course of Abia (Abijah), the 8th course, and both the Feast of Unleavened Bread (15-21 Nisan) and Pentecost (6 Sivan) would have occurred before his scheduled duty. This places Zacharias' administration in the Temple as beginning on the second Sabbath of the third month, Sivan (May-June).

Having completed his Temple service on the third Sabbath of Sivan, Zacharias returned home and soon conceived his son John. **So John the Baptist was probably conceived shortly after the third Sabbath of the month of Sivan.**

Now the reason that the information about John is important, is because according to Luke, Jesus was conceived by the Holy Spirit in the sixth month of Elizabeth's pregnancy:

Luke 1:24-27

[24] After these days Elizabeth his wife became pregnant, and she kept herself in seclusion for five months, saying, [25] "This is the way the Lord has dealt with me in the days when He looked *with favor* upon *me*, to take away my disgrace among men."

Jesus' Birth Foretold

[26] Now in the sixth month the angel Gabriel was sent from God to a city in Galilee called Nazareth, [27] to a virgin engaged to a man whose name was Joseph, of the descendants of David; and the virgin's name was Mary.

Note that verse 26 above refers to the sixth month of Elizabeth's pregnancy, not Elul, the sixth month of the Hebrew calendar, and this is made plain by the context of verse 24 and again in verse 36:

Luke 1:30-36

[30] The angel said to her, "Do not be afraid, Mary; for you have found favor with God. [31] And behold, you will conceive in your womb and bear a son, and you shall name Him Jesus. [32] He will be great and will be called the Son of the Most High; and the Lord God will give Him the throne of His father David; [33] and He will reign over the house of Jacob forever, and His kingdom will have no end." [34] Mary said to the angel, "How can this be, since I am a virgin?" [35] The angel answered and said to her, "The Holy Spirit will come upon you, and the power of the Most High will overshadow you; and for that reason the holy Child shall be called the Son of God. **[36] And behold, even your relative Elizabeth has also conceived a son in her old age; and she who was called barren is now in her sixth month.**

.Mary stayed with Elizabeth for the last 3 months of her pregnancy, until the time that John was born.

Luke 1:56-57–[56] And Mary stayed with her about three months, and *then* returned to her home.

John Is Born

[57] Now the time had come for Elizabeth to give birth, and she gave birth to a son.

Here is a table to help with the Jewish to Christian months

HOLY DAYS CALENDAR

MONTH	CHRISTIAN	DATE	HOLIDAY
NISAN	MARCH/APRIL	Nisan 14 Nisan 15-21 Nisan 16	Passover Unleavened Bread First Fruits
SIVAN	MAY/JUNE	Sivan 6	Shavuot (weeks) — —Pentecost
TISHRI	SEPT/OCT	Tishri 1 Tishri 10 Tishri 15-21	Rosh Hashannah — —Trumpets Yom Kipper Day of Atonement Tabernacles
KISLEV	NOV/DEC	Kislev 25 Tevet 2/3	Hanukkah

Working from the information about John's conception late in the third month, Sivan (May/June), and advancing six months, we arrive late in the 9th month of Kislev (Nov-Dec) **for the time frame for the *conception* of Jesus.** It is notable here that the first day of the Jewish festival of Hanukkah, the Festival of Lights, is celebrated on the 25th day of Kislev (Nov/Dec), and Jesus is called the light of the world.

John 8:12 Jesus Is the Light of the World Then Jesus again spoke to them, saying, "I am the Light of the world; he who follows Me will not walk in the darkness, but will have the Light of life."

10

John 9:5 While I am in the world, I am the Light of the world."

John 12:46 I have come *as* Light into the world, so that everyone who believes in Me will not remain in darkness.

This doesn't look like a coincidence. In the book of John, Hanukkah is called the feast of dedication. **John 10:22** At that time the Feast of the Dedication took place at Jerusalem;

Hanukkah–the feast of dedication–the feast of lights is an *eight* day festival of rejoicing, celebrating deliverance from enemies by the relighting of the menorah in the rededicated Temple, which according to the story, stayed lit miraculously for eight days on only one day's supply of oil.

When the Maccabees overtook the temple they had to rededicate it. To cleanse the temple they needed to light the candle for eight days. They only had oil for one day, but the candle stayed light for eight days. You can find the story in the "Book of Macabees" here is a look:

2 Maccabees 10 The Rededication of the Temple

10 ¹ Judas Maccabeus and his followers, under the leadership of the Lord, recaptured the Temple and the city of Jerusalem. ²They tore down the altars which foreigners had set up in the marketplace and destroyed the other places of worship that had been built. ³ They purified the Temple and built a new altar. Then, with new fire started by striking flint, they offered sacrifice for the first time in two years, burned incense, lighted the lamps, and set out the sacred loaves. ⁴After they had done all this, they lay face down on the ground and prayed that the Lord would never again let such disasters strike them. They begged him to be merciful when he punished

them for future sins and not hand them over any more to barbaric, pagan Gentiles. [5] They rededicated the Temple on the twenty-fifth day of the month of Kislev, the same day of the same month on which the Temple had been desecrated by the Gentiles. [6] The happy celebration lasted eight days, like the Festival of Shelters, and the people remembered how only a short time before, they had spent the Festival of Shelters wandering like wild animals in the mountains and living in caves. [7] But now, carrying green palm branches and sticks decorated with ivy, they paraded around, singing grateful praises to him who had brought about the purification of his own Temple. [8] Everyone agreed that the entire Jewish nation should celebrate this festival each year.

Based on a conception shortly after the third Sabbath of the month of Sivan, projecting forward an average term of about 10 lunar months (40 weeks), we arrive in the month of Nisan. It would appear that John the Baptist may have been born in the middle of the month, which would coincide with Passover and the Feast of Unleavened Bread. It is interesting to note, that even today, it is customary for the Jews to set out a special goblet of wine during the Passover Seder meal, in anticipation of the arrival of Elijah that week, which is based on the prophecy of Malachi:

Malachi 4:5–"Behold, I am going to send you Elijah the prophet before the coming of the great and terrible day of the LORD.

Jesus identified John as the "Elijah" that the Jews had expected:

Matthew 17:10-13–[10] And His disciples asked Him, "Why then do the scribes say that Elijah must come first?" [11] And He answered and said, "Elijah is coming and will restore all things; [12] but I say to you that Elijah already came, and they did not recognize him, but did to him whatever they wished. So also the Son of Man is going to suffer at their hands." [13] Then the disciples understood that He had spoken to them about John the Baptist.

The angel that appeared to Zacharias in the temple also indicated that John would be the expected "Eljah":

Luke 1:17—It is he who will go *as a forerunner* before Him in the spirit and power of Elijah, TO TURN THE HEARTS OF THE FATHERS BACK TO THE CHILDREN, and the disobedient to the attitude of the righteous, so as to make ready a people prepared for the Lord."

So then, the Feast of Unleavened Bread begins on the 15th day of the 1st month, Nisan (March/April), and this is a likely date for the birth of John the Baptist, the expected "Elijah".

The Birth of Jesus Christ.

Since Jesus was conceived six months after John the Baptist, and we have established a likely date for John's birth, we need only move six months farther down the Jewish calendar to arrive at a likely date for the birth of Jesus. From the 15th day of the 1st month, Nisan, we go to the 15th day of the **7th month, Tishri (Sept/Oct)**. And what do we find on that date? It is the **festival of Tabernacles**! The 15th day of Tishri begins the third and last festival of the year to which all the men of Israel were to gather in Jerusalem for Temple services.

Leviticus 23:34—"Speak to the sons of Israel, saying, 'On the fifteenth of this seventh month is the Feast of Booths for seven days to the LORD.

Isaiah 7:14–Therefore the Lord Himself will give you a sign: Behold, a virgin will be with child and bear a son, and she will call His name Immanuel.

Immanuel means "God with us". The Son of God had come to dwell with, or *tabernacle* on earth with His people.

John 1:14–The Word Made Flesh

[14] And the Word became flesh, and dwelt among us, and we saw His glory, glory as of the only begotten from the Father, full of grace and truth.

The Feast of Tabernacles (Sukkot), occurs five days after the Day of Atonement, and is a festival of rejoicing and celebration of deliverance from slavery in Egypt.

Leviticus 23:42-43–[42] You shall live in booths for seven days; all the native-born in Israel shall live in booths, [43] so that your generations may know that I had the sons of Israel live in booths when I brought them out from the land of Egypt. I am the LORD your God.'"

Luke 2:7-11–[7] And she gave birth to her firstborn son; and she wrapped Him in cloths, and laid Him in a manger, because there was no room for them in the inn.

[8] In the same region there were *some* shepherds staying out in the fields and keeping watch over their flock by night. [9] And an angel of the Lord suddenly stood before them, and the glory of the Lord shone around them; and they were terribly frightened. [10] But the angel said to them, "Do not be afraid; for behold, I bring you good news of great joy which will be for all the people; [11] for today in

the city of David there has been born for you a Savior, who is Christ the Lord.

Why was there no room at the inn? Bethlehem is only about 5 miles from Jerusalem, and all the men of Israel had come to the Temple in Jerusalem to attend the festival of Booths/Ingathering/Tabernacles as required by the law of Moses (Exodus 23:14-17, 34:22-23, Deuteronomy 16:16). Every room for miles around Jerusalem would have been already taken by pilgrims, so all that Mary and Joseph could find for shelter was a stable. During Tabernacles, everyone was to live in temporary booths (Sukkot), as a memorial to Israel's pilgrimage out of Egypt–Leviticus 23:42-43. The birth of the Savior, in what amounted to a temporary dwelling rather than a house, signaled the coming deliverance of God's people from slavery to sin, and their departing for the promised land, which is symbolized by Tabernacles.

So the birth of Jesus coincides with the "Feast of Tabernacles". God sent his son to "Tabernacle" with us!

Also, the Feast of Tabernacles is an *eight* day feast..

Leviticus 23:36, 39

[36] Each day for seven days you shall present a food offering. On the eighth day come together again for worship and present a food offering. It is a day for worship, and you shall do no work.

[39] When you have harvested your fields, celebrate this festival for seven days, beginning on the fifteenth day of the seventh month. The first day shall be a special day of rest.

Why eight days? It may be because an infant was dedicated to God by performing circumcision on the *eighth* day after birth: Medical scientists have been examining the processes that lead to blood clotting. . they found that two different blood clotting factors, Vitamin K and prothrombin are at the highest level of your life on the eighth day of life. How would the Israelites now this with out God's knowledge?

Luke 2:21– And when eight days had passed, before His circumcision, His name was *then* called Jesus, the name given by the angel before He was conceived in the womb.

So the infant Jesus would have been circumcised on the eighth and last day of the Feast of Tabernacles, a Sabbath day. The Jews today consider this a separate festival from Tabernacles, and they call it Shemini Atzeret.

The Baptism of Jesus–There is another indication in scripture as to when Jesus was born.

Mark 1:9-15–The Baptism of Jesus

[9] In those days Jesus came from Nazareth in Galilee and was baptized by John in the Jordan. [10] Immediately coming up out of the water, He saw the heavens opening, and the Spirit like a dove descending upon Him; [11] and a voice came out of the heavens: "You are My beloved Son, in You I am well-pleased." [12] Immediately the Spirit *impelled Him *to go* out into the wilderness. [13] And He was in the wilderness forty days being tempted by Satan; and He was with the wild beasts, and the angels were ministering to Him.

It is also very interesting to note that, after His baptism, Jesus went to synagogue. It was customary to read from the Law, the Prophets, and the writings. Jesus read from Isaiah -

Luke 4:16-21

[16] And He came to Nazareth, where He had been brought up; and as was His custom, He entered the synagogue on the Sabbath, and stood up to read. [17] And the book of the prophet Isaiah was handed to Him. And He opened the book and found the place where it was written,

[18] "THE SPIRIT OF THE LORD IS UPON ME,
BECAUSE HE ANOINTED ME TO PREACH THE GOSPEL TO THE POOR.
HE HAS SENT ME TO PROCLAIM RELEASE TO THE CAPTIVES,
AND RECOVERY OF SIGHT TO THE BLIND,
TO SET FREE THOSE WHO ARE OPPRESSED,
[19] TO PROCLAIM THE FAVORABLE YEAR OF THE LORD."

[20] And He closed the book, gave it back to the attendant and sat down; and the eyes of all in the synagogue were fixed on Him. [21] And He began to say to them, "Today this Scripture has been fulfilled in your hearing."

Jesus Preaches in Galilee

[14] Now after John had been taken into custody, Jesus came into Galilee, preaching the gospel of God, [15] and saying, "The time is fulfilled, and the kingdom of God is at hand; repent and believe in the gospel."

Jesus said **The time is fulfilled** just after His baptism, upon emerging from 40 days in the wilderness. He then began His preaching ministry, Luke tells us at about the age of 30.

Luke 3:22-23–²² and the Holy Spirit descended upon Him in bodily form like a dove, and a voice came out of heaven, "You are My beloved Son, in You I am well-pleased."

Genealogy of Jesus–²³ When He began His ministry, Jesus Himself was about thirty years of age, being, as was supposed, the son of Joseph, the son of Eli,

The book of Daniel gives us the "time" or prophecy Jesus was speaking about:

DANIEL'S 70 WEEKS

Daniel 9:24-27–Seventy Weeks and the Messiah

²⁴ "Seventy weeks have been decreed for your people and your holy city, to finish the transgression, to make an end of sin, to make atonement for iniquity, to bring in everlasting righteousness, to seal up vision and prophecy and to anoint the most holy *place*. ²⁵ So you are to know and discern *that* from the issuing of a decree to restore and rebuild Jerusalem (457 BC) until **Messiah the Prince *there will be* seven weeks and sixty-two weeks (69 weeks / 483 years, 27 A.D.**); it will be built again, with plaza and moat, even in times of distress. ²⁶ Then after the sixty-two weeks the Messiah will be cut off and have nothing, and the people of the prince who is to come will destroy the city and the sanctuary. And its end *will come* with a flood; even to the end there will be war; desolations are deter-mined. ²⁷ And he will make a firm covenant with the many for one week, but in the middle of the week (32AD) he will put a stop to sacrifice and grain offering; and on the wing of abominations *will come* one who makes desolate, even until a complete destruction, one that is decreed, is poured out on the one who makes desolate."

There is a longstanding tradition within Christianity of reading Daniel 9 as a messianic prophecy foretelling the coming of <u>Jesus Christ</u>. The seven and sixty-two-week "weeks" are most frequently understood as consecutive, making up a period of 96 weeks (483 years) beginning with the decree given to Ezra by Artaxerxes I in 457 BCE (the *terminus a quo*) and terminating with the baptism of Jesus. The reference to an anointed one being "cut off" in verse 26a is identified with the crucifixion of Jesus and has traditionally been thought to mark the midpoint of the seventieth week, which is also when Jeremiah's new "covenant" is "confirmed" (verse 27a) and atonement for "iniquity" (verse 24) is made. The "abomination that desolates" is typically read in the context of the New Testament references made to this expression in the Olivet Discourse

It is evident that by understanding this prophecy, and knowing the date of the decree when Daniel's 70 weeks began (Ezra 7, 457 B.C.), the wise men knew *exactly* when to look for the Christ child.

The "week" referred to here represents (primarily) a symbolic seven-year period. Thus once again, one day is made to signify one year. Here is why Daniel's "week" denotes seven years

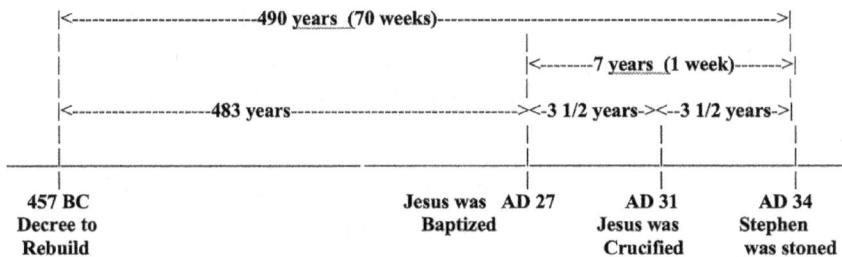

```
|<----------------------490 years  (70 weeks)--------------------------------------->|
|                                                     |                              |
|                                        |<--------7 years  (1 week)------->|         |
|                                        |            |                    |         |
|<------------------------483 years----------------------><-3 1/2 years-><--3 1/2 years->|
|                                        |            |          |         |
_____|_____|_____|_____|_____|_____
       |                                    |            |          |         |
  457 BC                               Jesus was  AD 27  AD 31              AD 34
  Decree to                            Baptized          Jesus was         Stephen
  Rebuild                                                Crucified         was stoned
```

This vision (of chapter 9) came to Daniel upon his understanding that the 70 years of Israelite exile (as prophesied by Jeremiah) had just elapsed:

19

Daniel 9:2– in the first year of his reign, I, Daniel, observed in the books the number of the years which was *revealed as* the word of the LORD to Jeremiah the prophet for the completion of the desolations of Jerusalem, *namely*, seventy years.

The Hebrew term for "weeks" is actually the plural of the word for "seven," without specifying whether it is days, months, or years;

Daniel's "seven-weeks" (49 days) can be understood symbolically as 49 years because of it's similarity with the seven weeks (49 days) till Pentecost; and the seven weeks of Pentecost follows the patters of the seven-times-seven years (49 years) of the Jubilee, (Deut. 16:9, Lev. 25:8).

The "dividing" of the last "week" of the 70 "weeks" is further explained in Daniel 12:9, where the 1290 days is mentioned. One-half ("dividing") of "one week" (i.e., of 7 years) amounts to this 1290 days; (i.e., 3.5 x 360 = 1260 days, + leap month = 1290 days). Hence, one "week" must symbolize years in order for half-a-week to total 1290 days (instead of a literal 3½ days).

> The 70th week of Daniel, a period of 7 literal years (a day equals a year), began with "Messiah the Prince". Messiah means anointed, and Jesus was publicly anointed by the Holy Spirit at His baptism, declaring him to be the Messiah, at the end of 69 weeks / 483 prophetic years, which calculates to 27 A.D. as the year of Christ's baptism.
>
> Knowing the year of Christ's baptism to be 483 years after the decree of Artaxerxes in 457 B.C., the wisemen needed simply to subtract 30 from 483 to know the Messiah would be born 453 years after the

decree. Why 30? A man had to be 30 years of age to serve in the Sanctuary / Temple (Num 4:3), and Luke says that at His baptism Jesus became about thirty. Jesus, when He turned 30, was considered to be old enough to perform the duties of a priest.

Daniel 9:26-27 also tells us that the Messiah would be "cut off" (crucified) in the "midst of the (70th) week". So 3 1/2 years after His baptism, which was at the end of 69 weeks / 483 prophetic years, on Tabernacles of 27 A.D., Jesus would be crucified, precisely on 14 Nisan, Passover of 31 A.D.

So, based on the scriptural evidence, a case can apparently be made that Jesus Christ was born on the 15th day of the month of Tishri, on the first day of the Feast of Tabernacles, which corresponds to the September–October timeframe of our present calendar!

It is also interesting to note that Tabernacles was a feast of ingathering of the Harvest (Exodus 23:16 and 34:22). If Jesus' first coming was indeed on 15 Tishri, the first day of Tabernacles, then it is quite reasonable to presume that the harvest of this earth, the ingathering of the second coming of Jesus Christ, will also occur on precisely the same date. The unknown factor would be the year that this would happen.

Jesus was born in a September/October time frame.

Scholars have debated about the truth of the first census since there is no record of it in the Roman archives. Their chief argument is that Augustus would not have imposed a census for the purpose of taxation in the kingdom of a client king like Herod. Herod had his own tax collectors and paid tribute to Rome from the proceeds. They further pose that the census in 6 CE was imposed because Herod's nutty son Archelaus had been deposed and Judea was placed under direct Roman rule.

The census of 6 CE therefore becomes the first census under direct Roman rule and fell in schedule with the Roman census on a 14 year rotation. The census of Jesus' birth, perhaps only a registration, became lost in the archives.

Chapter 3

PROPHECIES OF JESUS

❧

Against all odds, all prophecies of Jesus in the Bible have proven to be true. Some Bible scholars suggest there are more than 300 prophetic Scriptures completed in the life of Jesus. Circumstances such as his birthplace, lineage, and method of execution were beyond his control and could not have been accidentally or deliberately fulfilled.

In the book *Science Speaks*, Peter Stoner and Robert Newman discuss the statistical improbability of one man, whether accidentally or deliberately, fulfilling just eight of the prophecies Jesus fulfilled. The chance of this happening, they say, is 1 in 10^{17} power. The mathematical improbability of 300, or 44, or even just eight fulfilled prophesies of Jesus stands as evidence to his messiahship.

Prophecies of Jesus

You'll find 44 messianic predictions clearly fulfilled in Jesus Christ.

44 Messianic Prophecies of Jesus		
Prophecies about Jesus and fulfillment	**Scripture**	**Fulfillment**
1 Messiah would be born of a woman.	Genesis 3:15	Matthew 1:20 Galatians 4:4
2 Messiah would be born in Bethlehem.	Micah 5:2	Matthew 2:1 Luke 2:4-6
3 Messiah would be born of a virgin.	Isaiah 7:14	Matthew 1:22-23 Luke 1:26-31
4 Messiah would come from the line of Abraham.	Genesis 12:3 Genesis 22:18	Matthew 1:1 Romans 9:5
5 Messiah would be a descendant of Isaac.	Genesis 17:19 Genesis 21:12	Luke 3:34
6 Messiah would be a descendant of Jacob.	Numbers 24:17	Matthew 1:2
7 Messiah would come from the tribe of Judah.	Genesis 49:10	Luke 3:33 Hebrews 7:14
8 Messiah would be heir to King David's throne.	2 Samuel 7:12-13 Isaiah 9:7	Luke 1:32-33 Romans 1:3
9 Messiah's throne will be anointed and eternal.	Psalm 45:6-7 Daniel 2:44	Luke 1:33 Hebrews 1:8-12
10 Messiah would be called Immanuel.	Isaiah 7:14	Matthew 1:23
11 Messiah would spend a season in Egypt.	Hosea 11:1	Matthew 2:14-15
12 A massacre of children would happen at Messiah's birthplace.	Jeremiah 31:15	Matthew 2:16-18
13 A messenger would prepare the way for Messiah	Isaiah 40:3-5	Luke 3:3-6
14 Messiah would be rejected by his own people.	Psalm 69:8 Isaiah 53:3	John 1:11 John 7:5
15 Messiah would be a prophet.	Deuteronomy 18:15	Acts 3:20-22
16 Messiah would be preceded by Elijah.	Malachi 4:5-6	Matthew 11:13-14
17 Messiah would be declared the Son of God.	Psalm 2:7	Matthew 3:16-17

18	Messiah would be called a Nazarene.	Isaiah 11:1	Matthew 2:23
19	Messiah would bring light to Galilee.	Isaiah 9:1-2	Matthew 4:13-16
20	Messiah would speak in parables.	Psalm 78:2-4 Isaiah 6:9-10	Matthew 13:10-15, 34-35
21	Messiah would be sent to heal the brokenhearted.	Isaiah 61:1-2	Luke 4:18-19
22	Messiah would be a priest after the order of Melchizedek.	Psalm 110:4	Hebrews 5:5-6
23	Messiah would be called King.	Psalm 2:6 Zechariah 9:9	Matthew 27:37 Mark 11:7-11
24	Messiah would be praised by little children.	Psalm 8:2	Matthew 21:16
25	Messiah would be betrayed.	Psalm 41:9 Zechariah 11:12-13	Luke 22:47-48 Matthew 26:14-16
26	Messiah's price money would be used to buy a potter's field.	Zechariah 11:12-13	Matthew 27:9-10
27	Messiah would be falsely accused.	Psalm 35:11	Mark 14:57-58
28	Messiah would be silent before his accusers.	Isaiah 53:7	Mark 15:4-5
29	Messiah would be spat upon and struck.	Isaiah 50:6	Matthew 26:67
30	Messiah would be hated without cause.	Psalm 35:19 Psalm 69:4	John 15:24-25
31	Messiah would be crucified with criminals.	Isaiah 53:12	Matthew 27:38 Mark 15:27-28
32	Messiah would be given vinegar to drink.	Psalm 69:21	Matthew 27:34 John 19:28-30
33	Messiah's hands and feet would be pierced.	Psalm 22:16 Zechariah 12:10	John 20:25-27
34	Messiah would be mocked and ridiculed.	Psalm 22:7-8	Luke 23:35
35	Soldiers would gamble for Messiah's garments.	Psalm 22:18	Luke 23:34 Matthew 27:35-36
36	Messiah's bones would not be broken.	Exodus 12:46 Psalm 34:20	John 19:33-36

37	Messiah would be forsaken by God.	Psalm 22:1	Matthew 27:46
38	Messiah would pray for his enemies.	Psalm 109:4	Luke 23:34
39	Soldiers would pierce Messiah's side.	Zechariah 12:10	John 19:34
40	Messiah would be buried with the rich.	Isaiah 53:9	Matthew 27:57-60
41	Messiah would resurrect from the dead.	Psalm 16:10 Psalm 49:15	Matthew 28:2-7 Acts 2:22-32
42	Messiah would ascend to heaven.	Psalm 24:7-10	Mark 16:19 Luke 24:51
43	Messiah would be seated at God's right hand.	Psalm 68:18 Psalm 110:1	Mark 16:19 Matthew 22:44
44	Messiah would be a sacrifice for sin.	Isaiah 53:5-12	Romans 5:6-8

Sources

- ***100 Prophecies Fulfilled by Jesus: Messianic Prophecies Made Before the Birth of Christ** by Rose Publishing*
- *Book of Bible Lists by H.L. Willmington*
- *Story, D. (1997). Defending Your Faith (pp. 79-80)*
- *NKJV Study Bible*

Some very notable specifically accurate prophecies. Jesus would ride in on a donkey.

Zechariah 9:9–Rejoice greatly, O daughter of Zion! Shout *in triumph*, O daughter of Jerusalem! Behold, your king is coming to you; He is just and endowed with salvation, Humble, and mounted on a donkey, Even on a colt, the foal of a donkey. Jesus was born in Bethlehem

Micah 5:2–"But as for you, Bethlehem Ephrathah, *Too* little to be among the clans of Judah, From you One will go forth for Me to be ruler in Israel. His goings forth are from long ago, From the days of eternity." At His trial, Jesus did not open his mouth.

Isaiah 53:6-7–[6] All of us like sheep have gone astray, Each of us has turned to his own way; But the LORD has caused the iniquity of us all To fall on Him. [7] He was oppressed and He was afflicted, Yet He did not open His mouth; Like a lamb that is led to slaughter, And like a sheep that is silent before its shearers, So He did not open His mouth.

Daniel 9:24-27–Seventy Weeks and the Messiah

[24] "Seventy weeks have been decreed for your people and your holy city, to finish the transgression, to make an end of sin, to make atonement for iniquity, to bring in everlasting righteousness, to seal up vision and prophecy and to anoint the most holy *place*. [25] So you are to know and discern *that* from the issuing of a decree to restore and rebuild Jerusalem until Messiah the Prince *there will be* seven weeks and sixty-two weeks; it will be built again, with plaza and moat, even in times of distress. [26] Then after the sixty-two weeks the Messiah will be cut off and have nothing, and the people of the prince who is to come will destroy the city and the sanctuary. And its end *will come* with a flood; even to the end there will be war; desolations are determined. [27] And he will make a firm covenant with the many for one week, but in the middle of the week he will put a stop to sacrifice and grain offering; and on the wing of abominations *will come* one who makes desolate, even until a complete destruction, one that is decreed, is poured out on the one who makes desolate."

The starting date to restore and rebuild Jerusalem is found in Ezra. When was the decree to restore and rebuild Jerusalem issued?

This is somewhat debatable, as there are at least three "decrees" in the Book of Ezra. The first is in Ezra 1:1-4. This is a decree of Cyrus that the Jews can go back to Judah and Jerusalem and rebuild the temple. This decree is from about 537 BC. There is no mention of building the city, and especially of rebuilding the wall, which is almost the definition of a city back then, so this is probably not what the prophecy is a reference to.

The second "decree" is that of Darius in Ezra 6:1-12. This comes from about 518 BC. It is essentially a renewal of Cyrus' decree to rebuild the temple, and for the same reasons as above, this is probably not what the prophecy in Daniel 9 about a decree to restore and rebuild Jerusalem is referring to.

The third "decree" in Ezra is that of Artaxerxes in Ezra 7:11-28. This is a decree to actually rebuild the city. The decree comes from the seventh year of Artaxerxes (Ezra 7:8). This is somewhere around 458 BC from what we know of Artaxerxes' reign from outside sources. This decree actually resulted in the rebuilding of Jerusalem under Nehemiah.

So the time line in Daniel starts in 457 BC.

From 457 BC the next mark on the time line is 69 weeks. 1 prophetic day is equal to 1 literal year (Numbers 14:34 and Ezekiel 4:5,6) so 69 prophetic weeks is equal to 483 literal years. Starting at 457 BC and going forward 483 literal years is 27 AD. That is the date that Jesus was baptized.

Luke 3:21-22–Jesus Is Baptized

[21] Now when all the people were baptized, Jesus was also baptized, and while He was praying, heaven was opened, [22] and the

Holy Spirit descended upon Him in bodily form like a dove, and a voice came out of heaven, "You are My beloved Son, in You I am well-pleased."

In Luke we learn that John the Baptist was preaching and baptizing during the 15th year of Tiberius–27 AD. **Luke 3:1–John the Baptist Preaches**–Now in the fifteenth year of the reign of Tiberius Caesar, when Pontius Pilate was governor of Judea, and Herod was tetrarch of Galilee, and his brother Philip was tetrarch of the region of Ituraea and Trachonitis, and Lysanias was tetrarch of Abilene,

After Jesus was baptized, he spent 40 days and nights in the wilderness where he was tempted three times by the devil. After is time in the desert, he went to synagogue. **Luke 4:16-22** [16] And He came to Nazareth, where He had been brought up; and as was His custom, He entered the synagogue on the Sabbath, and stood up to read. [17] And the book of the prophet Isaiah was handed to Him. And He opened the book and found the place where it was written,

[18] "THE SPIRIT OF THE LORD IS UPON ME,
BECAUSE HE ANOINTED ME TO PREACH THE GOSPEL TO THE POOR.
HE HAS SENT ME TO PROCLAIM RELEASE TO THE CAPTIVES,
AND RECOVERY OF SIGHT TO THE BLIND,
TO SET FREE THOSE WHO ARE OPPRESSED,
[19] TO PROCLAIM THE FAVORABLE YEAR OF THE LORD."

[20] And He closed the book, gave it back to the attendant and sat down; and the eyes of all in the synagogue were fixed on Him. [21] And He began to say to them, "Today this Scripture has been fulfilled in your hearing." [22] And all were speaking well of Him, and wondering at the gracious words which were falling from His lips; and they were saying, "Is this not Joseph's son?"

The prophetic scripture (about himself) was from Isaiah. Isaiah 61:1–The Spirit of the Lord GOD is upon me, Because the LORD has anointed me To bring good news to the afflicted; He has sent me to bind up the brokenhearted, To proclaim liberty to captives And freedom to prisoners;

What follows next is a prophetic week, 7 years. Halfway through the week–3 1/2 years (31 AD) Jesus is crucified. Keeping with Daniels prophecy " he will put a stop to sacrifice and grain offering" Jesus did that with his sacrifice on the cross. **Matthew 27:33-51– The Crucifixion**

[33] And when they came to a place called Golgotha, which means Place of a Skull, [34] they gave Him wine to drink mixed with gall; and after tasting *it*, He was unwilling to drink.

[35] And when they had crucified Him, they divided up His garments among themselves by casting lots. [36] And sitting down, they *began* to keep watch over Him there. [37] And above His head they put up the charge against Him which read, "THIS IS JESUS THE KING OF THE JEWS."

[38] At that time two robbers *were crucified with Him, one on the right and one on the left. [39] And those passing by were hurling abuse at Him, wagging their heads [40] and saying, "You who *are going to* destroy the temple and rebuild it in three days, save Yourself! If You are the Son of God, come down from the cross." [41] In the same way the chief priests also, along with the scribes and elders, were mocking *Him* and saying, [42] "He saved others; He cannot save Himself. He is the King of Israel; let Him now come down from the cross, and we will believe in Him. [43] HE TRUSTS IN GOD; LET GOD RESCUE *Him* now, IF HE DELIGHTS IN HIM; for He said, 'I am the Son

of God.'" ⁴⁴The robbers who had been crucified with Him were also insulting Him with the same words.

⁴⁵Now from the sixth hour darkness fell upon all the land until the ninth hour. ⁴⁶About the ninth hour Jesus cried out with a loud voice, saying, "ELI, ELI, LAMA SABACHTHANI?" that is, "MY GOD, MY GOD, WHY HAVE YOU FORSAKEN ME?" ⁴⁷And some of those who were standing there, when they heard it, *began* saying, "This man is calling for Elijah." ⁴⁸Immediately one of them ran, and taking a sponge, he filled it with sour wine and put it on a reed, and gave Him a drink. ⁴⁹But the rest *of them* said, "Let us see whether Elijah will come to save Him." ⁵⁰And Jesus cried out again with a loud voice, and yielded up His spirit. ⁵¹And behold, the veil of the temple was torn in two from top to bottom; and the earth shook and the rocks were split.

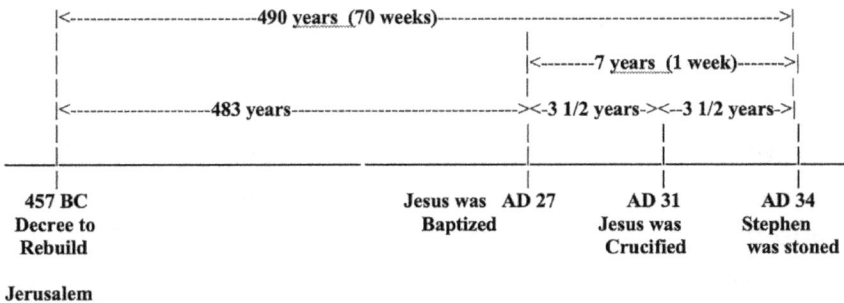

```
|<-----------------------490 years  (70 weeks)---------------------------------->|
|                                            |                                   |
|                                            |<--------7 years  (1 week)------->| |
|                                            |                                   |
|<---------------------483 years-------------------------><-3 1/2 years-><--3 1/2 years->|
|    |                                        |           |                     |
____|_____|_____|_____|____
    |                                        |           |                     |
 457 BC                              Jesus was  AD 27   AD 31               AD 34
 Decree to                             Baptized       Jesus was            Stephen
 Rebuild                                              Crucified            was stoned

Jerusalem
```

The final point on the 70 weeks time line is the Stoning of Stephen. Like the rest of the Bible, all of Acts 7 is a very good read. For brevity, I'll just include the Stoning of Stephen.

Acts 7:54-60–Stephen Put to Death

⁵⁴Now when they heard this, they were cut to the quick, and they *began* gnashing their teeth at him. ⁵⁵But being full of the Holy Spirit, he gazed intently into heaven and saw the glory of God, and

Jesus standing at the right hand of God; [56] and he said, "Behold, I see the heavens opened up and the Son of Man standing at the right hand of God." [57] But they cried out with a loud voice, and covered their ears and rushed at him with one impulse. [58] When they had driven him out of the city, they *began* stoning *him*; and the witnesses laid aside their robes at the feet of a young man named Saul. [59] They went on stoning Stephen as he called on *the Lord* and said, "Lord Jesus, receive my spirit!" [60] Then falling on his knees, he cried out with a loud voice, "Lord, do not hold this sin against them!" Having said this, he fell asleep.

A thought on the current prophecies–Jesus does not set foot on earth again until the "New Jerusalem" comes. When he comes to get those who believe in him, they meet him in the air. **1 Thessalonians 4:13-18** [13] **But** we do not want you to be uninformed, brethren, about those who are asleep, **so that you will not grieve as do the rest who have no hope.** [14] **For if we believe that Jesus died and rose again, even so** God will bring with Him those who have fallen asleep in Jesus. [15] **For this we say to you by the word of the Lord, that** we who are alive and remain until the coming of the Lord, will not precede those who have fallen asleep. [16] **For the Lord Himself will descend from heaven with a shout, with the voice of** *the* **archangel and with the trumpet of God, and the dead in Christ will rise first.** [17] **Then we who are alive and remain will be caught up together with them in the clouds to meet the Lord in the air, and so we shall always be with the Lord.** [18] **Therefore comfort one another with these words.**

Chapter 4

WHAT IS GOD'S NAME?

❦

G od told his name one time that was written in our Bible. He told it to Moses in Exodus.

Exodus 3:14 God said to Moses, "I AM WHO I AM"; and He said, "Thus you shall say to the sons of Israel, 'I AM has sent me to you.'"

This is the only time that the Hebrew pronunciation of GOD's name was in the Bible. The Hebrew people used "the Lord" or other titles like Adonai so that they would not inadvertently take the Lord's name in vane.

"I AM" in Hebrew is spelled "yod hey vav hey". In Hebrew it means "I AM" transliterate pronunciation is Y-H-V-H or like the sound of breath–Yohvah. In the Greek they used the "J" and it was pronounced Jehovah..

יהוה

Hebrew is read from Right to left. The letters above are YOD-HEY-VAV-HE (HE Sounds like Hey) So, the letters (right to left) are Y-H-V-H.

The Hebrew meaning is (I AM).

Exodus 3:14–God said "I AM THAT I AM"
Y-H-V-H Sounds like breath. Yehovah. or Yahweh Hebrew had no consonants. When the Greeks translated Hebrew the "H" became a "J" and Yehovah became Jehovah.
Also, Yeshua became known as Jesus.

WHAT IS GOD'S NAME?

Exodus 3:14–God said to Moses, "I AM WHO I AM"; and He said, "Thus you shall say to the sons of Israel, 'I AM has sent me to you.'"

PRIMARY NAMES OF GOD

יהוה
YAHWEH
I AM WHO I AM

השם
HASHEM
THE NAME

אלהים
ELOHIM
GOD THE CREATOR

אדני
ADONAI
LORD MASTER

אל
EL
THE
SOVEREIGN GOD

אלה
ELAH
THE AWESOME GOD

מלד
MELECH
THE KING

אבא
ABBA
DADDY

אבינו
AVINU
FATHER

Names of God
in The Old Testament

El Shaddai	Lord God Almighty
El Elyon	The Most High God
Adonai	Lord, Master
Yahweh	Lord, Jehovah
Jehovah Nissi	The Lord My Banner
Jehovah-Raah	The Lord My Shepherd
Jehovah Rapha	The Lord That Heals
Jehovah Shammah	The Lord is There
Jehovah Tsidkenu	The Lord Our Righteousness
Jehovah Mckoddishkem	The Lord Who Sanctifies You
El Olam	The Everlasting God
Elohim	God
Jehovah Jireh	The Lord Will Provide
Jehovah Shalom	The Lord Is Peace
Jehovah Sabaoth	The Lord of Hosts

What is the real name of God? YHVH, Jehovah, Yahweh?

Exodus 14-15 And God said to Moses, "I AM WHO I AM"; and He said, "Thus you shall say to the sons of Israel, `I AM has sent me to you.'" And God, furthermore, said to Moses, "Thus you shall say to the sons of Israel, `The Lord, the God of Abraham, the God of Isaac, and the God of Jacob, has sent me to you. This is My name forever, and this is My memorial-name to all generations."

To **transliterate** is to spell a word using the letters of another language. "I am" is the English translation of the meaning of God's personal name. The English transliteration of God's personal name is **YHVH**.

The four Hebrew letters transliterated **YHVH** are:

י –Yod, rhymes with "rode", which we transliterate "Y"

ה –He, rhymes with "say", which we transliterate "H"

ו –Vav, like "lava", which we transliterate "V"

ה –another He

Originally Hebrew (3000 years ago) didn't have any vowels, and was written right to left.

So to summarize.

God's name, as written in Hebrew right to left:

יהוה

Spelled left to right:

הוהי

Transliterated into English: **YHVH**

With vowels added: YAHWEH

Translated: **I AM WHO I AM**

The real name of God is YHVH, found in Exodus 3:14. However, there is no correct pronunciation for the name of God because the letters are only consonants, no vowels. I was once told by a Rabbi that GOD's name (YHVH) is only pronounced once a year in synagogue. So the "real" name of God is in **Exodus 3:13-14** it says, "Then Moses said to God, 'Behold, I am going to the sons of Israel, and I shall say to them, "The God of your fathers has sent

36

me to you." Now they may say to me, 'What is His name?' What shall I say to them?" And God said to Moses, "I AM WHO I AM"; and He said, "Thus you shall say to the sons of Israel, 'I AM has sent me to you.'"

When God says "I AM" he is speaking his name. In the Hebrew language that this verse was written in, the letters are yod, hey, vav, hey, from which we get YHVH. These four letters were very loosely translated into the English 'Jehovah.' However, there is no 'j' sound in the Hebrew. The Greeks used the "j" sound in their translation. So, a better approximation of the name of God would be Yahweh.

To reiterate, the pronunciation of God's name is difficult because when the Jews wrote His name in Hebrew Scriptures, they did not use vowel designations. They only used consonants. Therefore, the phrase "The name of God is YHVH". In English, The proper name of God is "I AM," which we transliterate into the English YHVH.

Light **IS**. Darkness is the absence of what is. And YHVH is light. YHVH IS. Light is. Darkness is not.

YHWH is life. Life, whatever it is, is. Death is simply the absence of life.

YHWH is light (energy/matter). Energy is. Light is just one form of energy.

YHWH is truth. Truth is a statement of what is. Falsehood is a statement of what is not.

"I AM THAT I AM." God is light, and in Him there is no darkness at all!

Why do Bibles use "LORD" instead of YHVH or Jehovah?

Bibles use "Lord" instead of YHVH or Jehovah because of the practice begun by the Jews hundreds of years before Christ. The Jews did not want to pronounce or mispronounce the name of YHVH out of reverence. They did not want to risk violating the commandment that says, "You shall not take the name of the Lord your God in vain, for the Lord will not leave him unpunished who takes His name in vain," **Exodus 20:7** "You shall not take the name of the LORD your God in vain, for the LORD will not leave him unpunished who takes His name in vain.

So, the Jews began substituting God's name (in Hebrew, "Lord") or Adonai. This practice is followed today in English translations of the Bible to show reverence for the Holy Name. Finally, since the early Hebrew text did not contain vowels but only consonants, it is not known exactly how to pronounce God's name. So, LORD is substituted for YHVH.

If someone were to write out God's name in English Bibles, what exactly would be the name?

In the Hebrew Old Testament, the word for "God" is Elohim. God is also called "Lord," which is translated in Hebrew Adonai. But, the special name of God that is given in **Exodus 3:14** is YHVH, which is "I AM."

Exodus 3:14, "And God said to Moses, "I AM WHO I AM"; and He said, "Thus you shall say to the sons of Israel, 'I AM has sent me to you.'"

The four letters YHVH are called the tetragrammaton and is sometimes written/pronounced Yahweh–a better pronunciation than

Jehovah since there is no "j" in Hebrew. The all capital LORD is the representation of YHVH, the personal name of God.

THE SEVEN–I AM–STATEMENTS OF JESUS

<u>I am the bread of life</u>

John 6:35, 48 [35] Jesus said to them, "**<u>I am</u>** the bread of life; he who comes to Me will not hunger, and he who believes in Me will never thirst. [48] **<u>I am</u>** the bread of life.

<u>I am the Light of the world</u>

John 8:12 Then Jesus again spoke to them, saying, "**<u>I am</u>** the Light of the world; he who follows Me will not walk in the darkness, but will have the Light of life."

<u>I am the Door</u>

John 10:1-2, 7-9

[1]"Truly, truly, I say to you, he who does not enter by the door into the fold of the sheep, but climbs up some other way, he is a thief and a robber. [2] But he who enters by the door is a shepherd of the sheep.

[7] So Jesus said to them again, "Truly, truly, I say to you, I am the door of the sheep. [8] All who came before Me are thieves and robbers, but the sheep did not hear them. [9] **<u>I am</u>** the door; if anyone enters through Me, he will be saved, and will go in and out and find pasture.

I am the Good Shepherd

John 10:11, 14

[11] "**I am** the good shepherd; the good shepherd lays down His life for the sheep. [14] **I am** the good shepherd, and I know My own and My own know Me,

I am the Resurrection and the Life

John 11:25 Jesus said to her, "**I am** the resurrection and the life; he who believes in Me will live even if he dies,

I am the Way, the Truth, and the Life

John 14:6 Jesus *said to him, "**I am** the way, and the truth, and the life; no one comes to the Father but through Me.

I am the True vine

John 15:1-5 [1]"**I am** the true vine, and My Father is the vinedresser. [2] Every branch in Me that does not bear fruit, He takes away; and every *branch* that bears fruit, He prunes it

From GOD in Exodus–Exodus 3:14

God said to Moses, "I AM WHO I AM"; and He said, "Thus you shall say to the sons of Israel, 'I AM has sent me to you.'"

About Jesus

John 8:58– Jesus said to them, "Truly, truly, I say to you, before Abraham was born, I am."

John 14:6– Jesus *said to him, "I am the way, and the truth, and the life; no one comes to the Father but through Me.

John 15:1-5–"I am the true vine, and My Father is the vine-dresser. Every branch in Me that does not bear fruit, He takes away; and every *branch* that bears fruit, He prunes it so that it may bear more fruit. You are already clean because of the word which I have spoken to you. Abide in Me, and I in you. As the branch cannot bear fruit of itself unless it abides in the vine, so neither *can* you unless you abide in Me. I am the vine, you are the branches; he who abides in Me and I in him, he bears much fruit, for apart from Me you can do nothing.

John 6:35-48– Jesus said to them, "I am the bread of life; he who comes to Me will not hunger, and he who believes in Me will never thirst. But I said to you that you have seen Me, and yet do not believe. All that the Father gives Me will come to Me, and the one who comes to Me I will certainly not cast out. For I have come down from heaven, not to do My own will, but the will of Him who sent Me. This is the will of Him who sent Me, that of all that He has given Me I lose nothing, but raise it up on the last day. For this is the will of My Father, that everyone who beholds the Son and believes in Him will have eternal life, and I Myself will raise him up on the last day."

John 8:12– Then Jesus again spoke to them, saying, "I am the Light of the world; he who follows Me will not walk in the darkness, but will have the Light of life."

John 9:5–While I am in the world, I am the Light of the world."

John 10:7– So Jesus said to them again, "Truly, truly, I say to you, I am the door of the sheep.

John 10:11-14– "I am the good shepherd; the good shepherd lays down His life for the sheep. He who is a hired hand, and not a shepherd, who is not the owner of the sheep, sees the wolf coming, and leaves the sheep and flees, and the wolf snatches them and scatters *them*. *He flees* because he is a hired hand and is not concerned about the sheep. I am the good shepherd, and I know My own and My own know Me,

John 11:25– Jesus said to her, "I am the resurrection and the life; he who believes in Me will live even if he dies,

John 8:24–Therefore I said to you that you will die in your sins; for unless you believe that I am *He*, you will die in your sins."

John 8:28– So Jesus said, "When you lift up the Son of Man, then you will know that I am *He*, and I do nothing on My own initiative, but I speak these things as the Father taught Me.

Chapter 5

THE SABBATH

∞

O ne of my biggest dilemmas has been the fact that the Day that God designated as Holy was changed from the Seventh day to the First day around the 4th century. Why did this happen and who did it?

In the very beginning, God designated the 7th day as Holy.
Genesis 2:1-3 Thus the heavens and the earth were finished, and all their multitude. [2] And on the seventh day God finished the work that he had done, and he rested on the seventh day from all the work that he had done. [3] So God blessed the seventh day and hallowed it, because on it God rested from all the work that he had done in creation. The seventh day. the Sabbath is the very first thing that God declared as being Holy

The 10 Commandments are found in Exodus 20:2–17 and Deuteronomy 5:6–21. Commandment number 4 is to remember the Sabbath Day – the 7th day – as described in Genesis. To give you an idea of how important Sabbath observance is Commandment number 4 is four verses long, Commandment 3 is three verses, all of the other commandments are only one verse in length.

Exodus 20:1–17

Then God spoke all these words: [2] I am the LORD your God, who brought you out of the land of Egypt, out of the house of slavery; [3] you shall have no other gods before (or besides) me.

[4] You shall not make for yourself an idol, whether in the form of anything that is in heaven above, or that is on the earth beneath, or that is in the water under the earth. [5] You shall not bow down to them or worship them; for I the LORD your God am a jealous God, punishing children for the iniquity of parents, to the third and the fourth generation of those who reject me, [6] but showing steadfast love to the thousandth generation of those who love me and keep my commandments.

[7] You shall not make wrongful use of the name of the LORD your God, for the LORD will not acquit anyone who misuses his name.

[8] Remember the Sabbath day, and keep it holy. [9] Six days you shall labor and do all your work. [10] But the seventh day is a Sabbath to the LORD your God; you shall not do any work— you, your son or your daughter, your male or female slave, your livestock, or the alien resident in your towns. [11] For in six days the LORD made heaven and earth, the sea, and all that is in them, but rested the seventh day; therefore the LORD blessed the Sabbath day and consecrated it.

[12] Honor your father and your mother, so that your days may be long in the land that the LORD your God is giving you.

[13] You shall not murder.

[14] You shall not commit adultery.

[15] You shall not steal.

[16] You shall not bear false witness against your neighbor.

[17] You shall not covet your neighbor's house; you shall not covet your neighbor's wife, or male or female slave, or ox, or donkey, or anything that belongs to your neighbor.

Exodus 31:12-17 The Sabbath Law

¹² The LORD said to Moses: ¹³ You yourself are to speak to the Israelites: "You shall keep my Sabbaths, for this is a sign between me and you throughout your generations, given in order that you may know that I, the LORD, sanctify you. ¹⁴ You shall keep the Sabbath, because it is holy for you; everyone who profanes it shall be put to death; whoever does any work on it shall be cut off from among the people. ¹⁵ Six days shall work be done, but the seventh day is a Sabbath of solemn rest, holy to the LORD; whoever does any work on the Sabbath day shall be put to death. ¹⁶ Therefore the Israelites shall keep the Sabbath, observing the Sabbath throughout their generations, as a perpetual covenant. ¹⁷ It is a sign forever between me and the people of Israel that in six days the LORD made heaven and earth, and on the seventh day he rested, and was refreshed."

Isaiah 58:13-14 Keeping the Sabbath

"If because of the Sabbath, you turn your foot From doing your *own* pleasure on My holy day, And call the Sabbath a delight, the holy *day* of the LORD honorable, And honor it, desisting from your own ways, From seeking your *own* pleasure And speaking *your own* word, Then you will take delight in the LORD, And I will make you ride on the heights of the earth; And I will feed you *with* the heritage of Jacob your father, For the mouth of the LORD has spoken."

Isaiah 48:18

"If only you had paid attention to My commandments! Then your well-being would have been like a river, And your righteousness like the waves of the sea.

SABBATH — the practice of observing one day in seven as a time for rest and worship originated in creation, because God created the universe in six days and rested on the seventh (Genesis 1). By this act, God ordained a pattern for living—that people should work six days each week at subduing and ruling the creation and should rest one day a week. This is the understanding of the creation set forth by Moses in Exodus 20:3–11, when God wrote the Ten Commandments in stone. By writing the Ten Commandments in stone, God let us know that His Laws were permanent.

Shabbat is the weekly day of rest in Judaism and Christianity, symbolizing the Seventh Day in the Book of Genesis, after six days of creation. In Judaism and some Christianity, it is observed from sundown on Friday until the appearance of three stars in the sky on Saturday night.

The principle of a weekly day of prayer and rest, derived from Shabbat, was eventually adopted and instituted by other religions as well. Constantine and the Catholic church moved observance of the Sabbath from Saturday to Sunday around the 4th century AD. Many 7th day Christian churches observe the Sabbath from Friday sunset to Saturday sunset as mentioned in Bible.
Muslims also keep the Sabbath in a manner which closely approximated the Jewish manner.

The Hebrew word Shabbat comes from the Hebrew verb *shavat*, which literally means "to cease." Although Shabbat ("Sabbath") is almost universally translated as "rest" or a "period of rest," a more literal translation would be "ceasing", with the implication of "ceasing from work." Thus, Shabbat is the day of ceasing from work.

The observance of Sabbath is mentioned many times in the Bible, most notably as the fourth of the Ten Commandments.

Exodus 20:8-11 [8] "Remember the Sabbath day, to keep it holy. [9] Six days you shall labor and do all your work, [10] but the seventh day is a Sabbath of the Lord your God; *in it* you shall not do any work, you or your son or your daughter, your male or your female servant or your cattle or your sojourner who stays with you. [11] For in six days the Lord made the heavens and the earth, the sea and all that is in them, and rested on the seventh day; therefore the Lord blessed the Sabbath day and made it holy.

Deuteronomy 5:12-15 [12] 'Observe the Sabbath day to keep it holy, as the Lord your God commanded you. [13] Six days you shall labor and do all your work, [14] but the seventh day is a Sabbath of the Lord your God; *in it* you shall not do any work, you or your son or your daughter or your male servant or your female servant or your ox or your donkey or any of your cattle or your sojourner who stays with you, so that your male servant and your female servant may rest as well as you. [15] You shall remember that you were a slave in the land of Egypt, and the Lord your God brought you out of there by a mighty hand and by an outstretched arm; therefore the Lord your God commanded you to observe the Sabbath day.

Exodus 31:12-17 The Sign of the Sabbath

[12] The Lord spoke to Moses, saying, [13] "But as for you, speak to the sons of Israel, saying, 'You shall surely observe My Sabbaths; for *this* is a sign between Me and you throughout your generations, that you may know that I am the Lord who sanctifies you. [14] Therefore you are to observe the Sabbath, for it is holy to you. Everyone who profanes it shall surely be put to death; for whoever does any work on it, that person shall be cut off from among his people. [15] For six days work may be done, but on the seventh day there is a Sabbath of complete rest, holy to the Lord; whoever does any work on the Sabbath day shall surely be put to death. [16] So the sons of Israel shall observe the Sabbath, to celebrate the sabbath throughout their generations as a perpetual covenant.' [17] It is a sign between Me and

the sons of Israel forever; for in six days the LORD made heaven and earth, but on the seventh day He ceased *from labor*, and was refreshed."

Exodus 35:2-3 [2] "For six days work may be done, but on the seventh day you shall have a holy *day*, a Sabbath of complete rest to the LORD; whoever does any work on it shall be put to death. [3] You shall not kindle a fire in any of your dwellings on the Sabbath day."

Leviticus 19:3, 30 [3] Every one of you shall reverence his mother and his father, and you shall keep My Sabbaths; I am the LORD your God. [30] You shall keep My Sabbaths and revere My sanctuary; I am the LORD.

Leviticus 23:3 'For six days work may be done, but on the seventh day there is a Sabbath of complete rest, a holy convocation. You shall not do any work; it is a Sabbath to the LORD in all your dwellings.

Isaiah 56:4-6 For thus says the LORD,

"To the eunuchs who keep My Sabbaths,
And choose what pleases Me,
And hold fast My covenant,
[5] To them I will give in My house and within My walls a memorial,
And a name better than that of sons and daughters;
I will give them an everlasting name which will not be cut off.

[6] "Also the foreigners who join themselves to the LORD,
To minister to Him, and to love the name of the LORD,
To be His servants, every one who keeps from profaning the Sabbath
And holds fast My covenant;

Nehemiah 9:14 "So You made known to them Your holy Sabbath, And laid down for them commandments, statutes and law, Through Your servant Moses.

There are several witnesses for the Sabbath. **Deuteronomy 19:15** "A single witness shall not rise up against a man on account of any iniquity or any sin which he has committed; on the evidence of two or three witnesses a matter shall be confirmed.

Judaism accords Shabbat the status of a joyous holy day. Shabbat Shalom means Sabbath Peace.

The practice of the weekly Sabbath is suggested at several places in the Bible, long before the Ten Commandments were given at Mt. Sinai. In Genesis, for example, starting with Seth **Genesis 4:26** To Seth, to him also a son was born; and he called his name Enosh. Then *men* began to call upon the name of the LORD.

(Gen. 4:26), To Seth, to him also a son was born; and he called his name Enosh. Then men began to call upon the name of the Lord in acts of worship. Periods of seven days play a prominent role at crucial points throughout Genesis

Genesis 7:4,10 [4] For after seven more days, I will send rain on the earth forty days and forty nights; and I will blot out from the face of the land every living thing that I have made." [10] It came about after the seven days, that the water of the flood came upon the earth. **Genesis 8:10-12** [10] So he waited yet another seven days; and again he sent out the dove from the ark. [11] The dove came to him toward evening, and behold, in her beak was a freshly picked olive leaf. So Noah knew that the water was abated from the earth. [12] Then he waited yet another seven days, and sent out the dove; but she did not return to him again.

The mention of a seven-day week and a seven-year cycle in the life practice of Laban, Abraham's relative, is striking.

The Old Testament prophets recounted God's blessings upon those who properly observed the Sabbath **Isaiah 58:13** "If because of the Sabbath, you turn your foot From doing your *own* pleasure on My holy day, And call the Sabbath a delight, the holy *day* of the LORD honorable, And honor it, desisting from your *own* ways, From seeking your *own* pleasure And speaking *your own* word, They called upon the people to observe the Sabbath (Neh. 10:31; 13:15–22), while soundly condemning those who made much of external observance and ignored the heart and moral issues to which the Sabbath bound them (Is. 1:13; Hos. 2:11; Amos 8:5). During the period between the Old and New Testaments, Jewish religious leaders added greatly to the details of Sabbath legislation. They sought to insure proper and careful observance by making certain that people did not even come close to violating it. This substituted human law for divine law, **Matthew 15:9** 'BUT IN VAIN DO THEY WORSHIP ME, TEACHING AS DOCTRINES THE PRECEPTS OF MEN.'" This made the law a burden rather than a rest and delight (Luke 11:46), and reduced the Sabbath to little more than an external observance (Matt. 12:8). Jesus, like the Old Testament prophets, kept the Sabbath Himself **Luke 4:16** And He came to Nazareth, where He had been brought up; and as was His custom, He entered the synagogue on the Sabbath, and stood up to read. and urged others to observe the day. **Mark 2:28** So the Son of Man is Lord even of the Sabbath." But He condemned the pharisaical attitude that missed the deep spiritual truth behind Sabbath observance (Matt 12:14; Mark 2:23; Luke 6:1–11; John 5:1–18).

The Christian Sabbath. Rather than following the Bible, Many Christians feel that the Sabbath was changed to the first day.

Historically, the Sabbath was changed to Sunday by Emperor Constantine I—a pagan sun-worshipper— he came to power in A.D. 313, he legalized Christianity and made the first Sunday-keeping law. His infamous Sunday enforcement law of March 7, A.D. 321. This was prophesized in Daniel. **Daniel 7:25** He will speak out against the Most High and wear down the saints of the Highest One, and he will intend to make alterations in times and in law; and they will be given into his hand for a time, times, and half a time. **Deuteronomy 4:2** You shall not add to the word which I am commanding you, nor take away from it, that you may keep the commandments of the LORD your God which I command you **Revelation 22:18-19** [18] I testify to everyone who hears the words of the prophecy of this book: if anyone adds to them, God will add to him the plagues which are written in this book; [19] and if anyone takes away from the words of the book of this prophecy, God will take away his part from the tree of life and from the holy city, which are written in this book. **Hebrews 13:8** Jesus Christ *is* the same yesterday and today and forever.

God's word could not be plainer. God's word does not change

Hebrews 13:8 Jesus Christ *is* the same yesterday and today and forever.

The Sabbath is Saturday (the 7th day) and has never changed. In fact it is a sin to change God's word.

Christians usually observe Sunday, the first day of the week, as the Christian Sabbath. They note that Christ arose on the first day of the week **Matthew 28:1 Jesus Is Risen!** Now after the Sabbath, as it began to dawn toward the first day of the week, Mary Magdalene and the other Mary came to look at the grave.

and, thereafter, some Christians falsely assume that the New Testament church regularly worshiped on Sunday. If the New Christians, at the time, had worshipped on Sunday, rather than the Sabbath, they would have been kicked out of the church and the preaching's of Jesus would have meant nothing.

Jesus was crucified, was dead and buried on a Friday. Rested on the Sabbath and was resurrected on Sunday, the first day. What does the Bible say about the first day? **Acts 20:7** On the first day of the week, when we were gathered together to break bread, Paul *began* talking to them, intending to leave the next day, and he prolonged his message until midnight.

1 Corinthians 16:2 On the first day of every week each one of you is to put aside and save, as he may prosper, so that no collections be made when I come.

in observance of the Sabbath (Saturday) no money was to change hands.

Modern day Christians often confuse scripture. **Revelation 1:10** I was in the Spirit on the Lord's day, and I heard behind me a loud voice like *the sound* of a trumpet,

The Lord's day is the Sabbath–**Matthew 12:8 Lord of the Sabbath**

[8] For the Son of Man is Lord of the Sabbath."

Luke 6:1-11 Jesus Is Lord of the Sabbath

6 Now it happened that He was passing through *some* grainfields on a Sabbath; and His disciples were picking the heads of grain, rubbing them in their hands, and eating *the grain*. [2] But some of the

Pharisees said, "Why do you do what is not lawful on the Sabbath?" [3] And Jesus answering them said, "Have you not even read what David did when he was hungry, he and those who were with him, [4] how he entered the house of God, and took and ate the consecrated bread which is not lawful for any to eat except the priests alone, and gave it to his companions?" [5] And He was saying to them, "The Son of Man is Lord of the Sabbath."

[6] On another Sabbath He entered the synagogue and was teaching; and there was a man there whose right hand was withered. [7] The scribes and the Pharisees were watching Him closely *to see* if He healed on the Sabbath, so that they might find *reason* to accuse Him. [8] But He knew what they were thinking, and He said to the man with the withered hand, "Get up and come forward!" And he got up and came forward. [9] And Jesus said to them, "I ask you, is it lawful to do good or to do harm on the Sabbath, to save a life or to destroy it?" [10] After looking around at them all, He said to him, "Stretch out your hand!" And he did *so*; and his hand was restored. [11] But they themselves were filled with rage, and discussed together what they might do to Jesus.

The Lord's Day is The Sabbath! Look at the crucifixion. Jesus was crucified on Friday. He rested on the Sabbath, and Rose early the first day (Sunday Morning).

This day on which Jesus arose was falsely called the LORD'S DAY (Rev. 1:10). It was the first day, not the Lord's day. Nowhere is this mentioned in the Bible, Jesus does say that he is the Lord of the Sabbath. Jesus, and all of the disciples kept Saturday as the Sabbath. **Luke 4:16** And He came to Nazareth, where He had been brought up; and as was His custom, He entered the synagogue on the Sabbath, and stood up to read.

53

A few Christian groups, however, deny that observance of the seventh day as the Sabbath was ever abolished. Among them are Seventh-Day Adventists and Seventh-Day Baptists. Sabbath was kept as the 7th day (Saturday) until the 4th century when it was changed by Constantine and the catholic church. The Sabbath is a means by which our living pattern imitates God's (Ex. 20:3–11). Work is followed by rest. This idea is expressed by the Hebrew word for Sabbath, which means "cessation."

Sabbath rest is also a time for God's people to think about and enjoy what God has accomplished. Another Hebrew word meaning "rest" embodies this idea, "But the seventh day is the Sabbath of the LORD your God. In it you shall not do any work," (Deut. 5:14). Sabbath rest also holds promise of the ultimate salvation that God will accomplish for His people. As certainly as He delivered them from Egypt through Moses, so will He deliver His people from sin at the end of the age through the Great Redeemer (Gen. 3:15; Hebrews 4).

Finally, the Sabbath includes the idea and practice of celebrating rest, or salvation. To this end, God declared that His Sabbath was a day for public convocation (Lev. 23:3; Ex. 31:13; Ezek. 20:12).

The concept of celebration also presents the Sabbath as a delight (Ps. 92; Is. 58:13; Hos. 2:11). The sabbatical holy days (holidays) prescribed rest from work for everyone (Ex. 23:21; Num. 15:32). On the Sabbath the SHOWBREAD was to be renewed (Lev. 24:8). The people were to meet together to praise God and to be instructed in His law (Lev. 10:11; Deut. 14:29; 33:10).

Saturday–The seventh day of the week.

The three Abrahamic religions, via their original languages, regard Saturday as the seventh day of the week (Judaism via Hebrew,

Christianity via Ecclesiastical Latin, and Islam via Arabic) by naming Monday, Tuesday, Wednesday, and Thursday as the second through fifth days of the week. This is concordant with the European Pagan tradition, which named the days of the week after the seven Classical planets (in order Sun, Moon, Mars, Mercury, Jupiter, Venus, Saturn), naming the first day of the week for the Sun, in a way of honoring their sun god.

Isaiah 66:23 "And it shall be from new moon to new moon And from Sabbath to Sabbath, All mankind will come to bow down before Me," says the LORD.

Chapter 6

THE SAPPHIRE THRONE AND THE TEN COMMANDMENTS

∽

T he Bible tells us the spiritual meaning of the color blue:

Numbers 15:38-40 [38] "Speak to the sons of Israel, and tell them that they shall make for themselves tassels on the corners of their garments throughout their generations, and that they shall put on the tassel of each corner a cord of blue. [39] It shall be a tassel for you to look at and remember all the commandments of the LORD, so as to do them and not follow after your own heart and your own eyes, after which you played the harlot, [40] so that you may remember to do all My commandments and be holy to your God.

In Numbers 15, the context for the blue tassels or ribbands is intentional sinning **Numbers 15:30-31** [30] But the person who does *anything* defiantly, whether he is native or an alien, that one is blaspheming the LORD; and that person shall be cut off from among his people. [31] Because he has despised the word of the LORD and has broken His commandment, that person shall be completely cut off; his guilt *will be* on him.'" and breaking the Sabbath commandment **Numbers 15:32-36 Sabbath-breaking Punished** [32] Now while the sons of Israel were in the wilderness, they found a man gathering wood on the Sabbath day. [33] Those who found him gathering wood brought him to Moses and Aaron and to all the congregation; [34] and they put him in custody because it had not been declared what should be done to him. [35] Then the LORD said to Moses, "The man shall surely be put to death; all the congregation shall stone him with stones outside the camp." [36] So all the congregation brought him outside the camp and stoned him to death with stones, just as the LORD had commanded Moses.

Note that there is no mention of repentance by the man who was gathering sticks, he was breaking the Sabbath intentionally in open defiance of the law. For that he was put to death. This practice of blue in tassels survives today in the Jewish prayer shawl, known as a tallit. The tassel with the ribband of blue on the four corners of the tallit is called a tzitzit.

The color blue goes back to MOUNT SINAI. It is understood that the tablets of the Ten Commandments were cut from the clear blue sapphire seen on mount Sinai. When Moses ascended mount Sinai it was of sapphire stone;

Exodus 24:10 and they saw the God of Israel; and under His feet there appeared to be a pavement of sapphire, as clear as the sky itself.

Sapphire makes up the very throne of God; **Ezekiel 1:26** Now above the expanse that was over their heads there was something resembling a throne, like lapis lazuli in appearance; and on that which resembled a throne, high up, was a figure with the appearance of a man.

Dictionary–lap·is laz·u·li NOUN a bright blue metamorphic rock consisting largely of lazurite, used for decoration and in jewelry. synonyms: sky blue · azure · cobalt (blue) · **sapphire** · cerulean · navy (blue) · saxe (blue) · Oxford blue · Cambridge blue · ultramarine · lapis lazuli · indigo

Ezekiel 10:1 Then I looked, and behold, in the expanse that was over the heads of the cherubim something like a sapphire stone, in appearance resembling a throne, appeared above them.

So, the Ark of the Covenant in the most holy apartment of the sanctuary, the throne of God's presence (the Shekinah glory), contained the blue sapphire tablets of the Ten Commandments.

Hence why the Ten Commandments are blue.

THE BLUE SKY

Have you wondered why the sky is blue? God has placed objects in nature for our learning. If you walk outside right now and take a look at that sky from horizon to horizon you'll see that its blue and this refers to the fact that God has provided perfection for every person that has ever lived on this earth. If you read Numbers 23:21. When Balaam was going to curse but he opened his mouth and blessed and said, There is no sin in Jacob, there is no iniquity in Israel. **Numbers 23:21** "He has not observed misfortune in Jacob; Nor has He seen trouble in Israel; The LORD his God is with him,

And the shout of a king is among them.

There were two and a half million people camped down in the Jordan Valley. God looked down on that whole camp of two and a half million people. He said, I saw no iniquity. I saw no sin in

Israel. Is that true? No. Why, there were sinners in there' and they crossed the Jordan and they were still sinners.

Why did God say that? That there was no sin and no iniquity in Israel? Because God had provided a blue covering of this particular skirt over all the people. Now it's up to them to find that out, and accept it in their mind, but the provision had already been made.

CAIAPHAS

Now, Caiaphas, to get a conviction against Christ, asked him if he was the son of God. Jesus said, You have just so declared.

Caiaphas, the high priest, got so mad, he ripped this robe which was totally blue and it was the perfection that God provided for Israel and all the world. When he tore that garment, he tore the righteousness of Christ off from his life, and as high priest he tore it off from the whole Hebrew nation. And they have not come under that blue garment until this very day as a people. Now they may do so as individuals, but as a nation they have not made that decision. **Matthew 26:65** Then the high priest tore **his clothes** and said, "He has spoken blasphemy! Why do we need any more witnesses? Look, now you have heard the blasphemy.

An ephod was a shawl or wrap, for the High Priest it was a particular outer garment in the style of a tunic or pinafore. It was made of linen in **blue**, purple, and scarlet and there was golden threads woven into it. It was made in two pieces joined together at the shoulders with golden clasps. Each clasp was set with an engraved onyx stone.

Malachi 4:2 "But for you who fear My name, the sun of righteousness will rise with healing in its wings; and you will go forth and skip about like calves from the stall.

So what does healing in his wings mean? The word translated "wings" is an edge or extremity; spec. (of a bird or army) a wing, (of a garment or bed-clothing).

Malachi was really saying that the Messiah would have healing in the edge or fringe of His garment. This was what was understood by the people of Israel. How do we know that? **Matthew 14:35-36** [35] And when the men of that place recognized Him, they sent word into all that surrounding district and brought to Him all who were sick; [36] and they implored Him that they might just touch the fringe of His cloak; and as many as touched it were cured.

Matthew 9:20-22 [20] And a woman who had been suffering from a hemorrhage for twelve years, came up behind Him and touched the fringe of His cloak; [21] for she was saying to herself, "If I only touch His garment, I will get well." [22] But Jesus turning and seeing her said, "Daughter, take courage; your faith has made you well." At once the woman was made well.

See also Mark 5:25-34 and Luke 8:43-48.

The fringe or tassel of Christ's garment undoubtedly included the sapphire blue ribband as directed in Numbers 15:38-39 that symbolized the commandments of God. That is why the woman sought so earnestly to touch that hem or fringe. She knew Malachi's prophecy, and in faith she made her way through the crowd to claim that healing.

Numbers 15:38-40 [38] "Speak to the sons of Israel, and tell them that they shall make for themselves tassels on the corners of their garments throughout their generations, and that they shall put on the tassel of each corner a cord of blue. [39] It shall be a tassel for you to look at and remember all the commandments of the LORD, so as to do them and not follow after your own heart and your own eyes, after which you played the harlot, [40] so that you may remember to do all My commandments and be holy to your God.

Chapter 7

WHO CHANGED THE SABBATH TO SUNDAY

≈

There is no doubt that Christ, His disciples, and the first-century Christians kept Saturday, the seventh-day Sabbath. Yet, today, most of the world that claims to be Christians keeps Sunday, the first day of the week, calling it the Sabbath. Who made this change, and how did it occur?

If you seriously study the Scriptures you know that God created the Sabbath at creation and blessed the seventh day as holy' **Genesis 2:2-3** ² By the seventh day God completed His work which He had done, and He rested on the seventh day from all His work which He had done. ³ Then God blessed the seventh day and sanctified it, because in it He rested from all His work which God had created and made.

It was later written in stone–put in stone–by God as the Fourth Commandment **Exodus 20:8-11** ⁸ "Remember the Sabbath day, to keep it holy. ⁹ Six days you shall labor and do all your work, ¹⁰ but the seventh day is a Sabbath of the LORD your God; in it you shall not do any work, you or your son or your daughter, your male or your female servant or your cattle or your sojourner who stays with you. [11] For in six days the LORD made the heavens and the earth, the sea and all that is in them, and rested on the seventh day; therefore the LORD blessed the Sabbath day and made it holy.

God's word makes it clear that Sabbath observance is a special sign between God and His people. It's very clear that Christ, His disciples, and the first-century Christians (and probably the second and third century Christians) kept the seventh-day Sabbath as commanded—the day we call "Saturday"

Mark 2:28 So the Son of Man is Lord even of the Sabbath."

Luke 4:16 And He came to Nazareth, where He had been brought up; and as was His custom, He entered the synagogue on the Sabbath, and stood up to read.

There is absolutely *no* New Testament text stating that God, Jesus, or the apostles changed the Sabbath to Sunday—not a text, not a word, not even a hint or suggestion. *If* there were, those chapters and verses would be loudly shouted by those against a Saturday Sabbath. If Paul or any other apostle taught a change from Sabbath to Sunday, the first day of the week, the conservative Jewish Christians would have let everyone know and have been protesting. The Pharisees and scribes would have insisted that Paul or any other person even suggesting such a thing be stoned to death for the sin of Sabbath-breaking. This would have been a much larger issue than the controversy over circumcision!

The Pharisees had already falsely accused Christ of breaking the Sabbath because He violated the added man-made rules and traditions they placed upon the Sabbath. **Mark 2:24** The Pharisees were saying to Him, "Look, why are they doing what is not lawful on the Sabbath?"

The fact that nothing was ever said or written about a change in the day of worship is one of the best evidences showing the apostles and other New Testament Christians did not change the day. On the contrary, we have a record of many Sabbaths that Paul and his traveling companions kept long after the resurrection of Jesus Christ.

Acts 13:14,27,42-44

[14] But going on from Perga, they arrived at Pisidian Antioch, and on the Sabbath day they went into the synagogue and sat down.. [27] For those who live in Jerusalem, and their rulers, recognizing neither Him nor the utterances of the prophets which are read every Sabbath, fulfilled *these* by condemning *Him*. [42] As Paul and Barnabas were going out, the people kept begging that these things might be spoken to them the next Sabbath. [43] Now when *the meeting of* the synagogue had broken up, many of the Jews and of the God-fearing proselytes followed Paul and Barnabas, who, speaking to them, were urging them to continue in the grace of God. [44] The next Sabbath nearly the whole city assembled to hear the word of the Lord.

Acts 15:21 For Moses from ancient generations has in every city those who preach him, since he is read in the synagogues every Sabbath."

Acts 16:13 And on the Sabbath day we went outside the gate to a riverside, where we were supposing that there would be a place of prayer; and we sat down and began speaking to the women who had assembled.

Acts 17:2 And according to Paul's custom, he went to them, and for three Sabbaths reasoned with them from the Scriptures,

Acts 13:42-44 is especially important–. [42] As Paul and Barnabas were going out, the people kept begging that these things might be spoken to them the next Sabbath. [43] Now when *the meeting of* the synagogue had broken up, many of the Jews and of the God-fearing proselytes followed Paul and Barnabas, who, speaking to them, were urging them to continue in the grace of God. [44] The next Sabbath nearly the whole city assembled to hear the word of the Lord.

Paul and Barnabas were speaking at a Jewish synagogue and were invited to speak again the next Sabbath. Paul could have asked them to meet with him the next day rather than waiting a whole week for the Sabbath. But, on The next Sabbath nearly the whole city (Jews and gentiles alike) assembled to hear the word of the Lord.

Yet today, most of the Christian world keeps Sunday, the first day of the week, calling it the Sabbath. So, who changed the Sabbath to Sunday. When and how did it occur?

The New Testament clearly shows that we are to keep the commandments.

Matthew 5:17-18 [17] "Do not think that I came to abolish the Law or the Prophets; I did not come to abolish but to fulfill. [18] For truly I say to you, until heaven and earth pass away, not the smallest letter or stroke shall pass from the Law until all is accomplished.

Matthew 19:17 And He said to him, "Why are you asking Me about what is good? There is *only* One who is good; but if you wish to enter into life, keep the commandments."

65

Matthew 28:20 teaching them to observe all that I commanded you; and lo, I am with you always, even to the end of the age."

So, Where does man get the authority to change the fourth commandment from Sabbath to Sunday?

Many centuries earlier, Daniel prophesied that a time would come when man would think to changes times and laws.

Daniel 7:25 He will speak out against the Most High and wear down the saints of the Highest One, and he will intend to make alterations in times and in law; and they will be given into his hand for a time, times, and half a time.

The Christians kept the Sabbath on the correct day, the seventh day of the week, from about 35 to 100 A.D. For the first 300 years of Christian history, Roman Emperors thought of themselves as gods and Christianity became an illegal religion. God's people were scattered abroad.

Acts 8:1 Saul Persecutes the Church Saul was in hearty agreement with putting him to death. (Stephen) And on that day a great persecution began against the church in Jerusalem, and they were all scattered throughout the regions of Judea and Samaria, except the apostles.

From A.D. 70 to A.D. 135 Sunday was a day of rest of the Roman empire.. The Roman religion was Mithraism a form of sun worship.

During the Empire-wide persecutions under Nero, Maximin, Diocletian, and Galerius, Sabbath keeping Christians were hunted down, tortured, and for sport, often used for entertainment in the Coliseum.

When Emperor Constantine I — a pagan sun-worshipper — came to power in A.D. 313, he legalized Christianity and made the first Sunday-keeping law. His infamous Sunday enforcement law of March 7, A.D. 321, reads as follows: "On the venerable Day of the Sun let the magistrates and people residing in cities rest, and let all workshops be closed." (*Codex Justinianus* 3.12.3, trans. Philip Schaff, *History of the Christian Church*, 5th ed. (New York, 1902), 3:380, note 1.)

The Sunday law was officially confirmed by the Roman Papacy. The Council of Laodicea in A.D. 364 decreed, "Christians shall not Judaize and be idle on Saturday but shall work on that day; but the Lord's day they shall especially honor, and, as being Christians, shall, if possible, do no work on that day. If, however, they are found Judaizing, they shall be shut out from Christ" (Strand, *op. cit.,* citing Charles J. Hefele, *A History of the Councils of the Church*, 2 [Edinburgh, 1876] 316).

Cardinal Gibbons, in *Faith of Our Fathers*, 92nd ed., p. 89, freely admits, "You may read the Bible from Genesis to Revelation, and you will not find a single line authorizing the sanctification of Sunday. The Scriptures enforce the religious observance of Saturday, a day which we [the Catholic Church] never sanctify."

Again, "The Catholic Church, ... by virtue of her divine mission, changed the day from Saturday to Sunday" (*The Catholic Mirror*, official publication of James Cardinal Gibbons, Sept. 23, 1893).

"Protestants do not realize that by observing Sunday, they accept the authority of the spokesperson of the Church, the Pope" (*Our Sunday Visitor*, February 5, 1950).

"Of course the Catholic Church claims that the change [Saturday Sabbath to Sunday] was her act... And the act is a mark of her ecclesiastical authority in religious things" (H.F. Thomas, Chancellor of Cardinal Gibbons).

"Sunday is our mark of authority... the church is above the Bible, and this transference of Sabbath observance is proof of that fact" (Catholic Record of London, Ontario Sept 1, 1923).

What a shocking admission!

Again, lets remember the amazing prophecy of Daniel.

Daniel 7:25 He will speak out against the Most High and wear down the saints of the Highest One, and he will intend to make alterations in times and in law; and they will be given into his hand for a time, times, and half a time.

Adam Clarke's Commentary on the Bible says:

"He shall speak great words against the Most High. Literally, Sermones quasi Deus loquetur; "He shall speak as if he were God." So Jerome quotes from Symmachus. To none can this apply so well or so fully as to the popes of Rome. They have assumed infallibility, which belongs only to God. They profess to forgive sins, which belongs only to God. They profess to open and shut heaven, which belongs only to God. They profess to be higher than all the kings of the earth, which belongs only to God. And they go beyond God in pretending to loose whole nations from their oath of allegiance to their kings, when such kings do not please them! And they go against God when they give indulgences for sin. This is the worst of all blasphemies!

And shall wear out the saints. By wars, crusades, massacres, inquisitions, and persecutions of all kinds. What in this way have they not done against all those who have protested against their innovations, and refused to submit to their idolatrous worship? Witness the exterminating crusades published against the Waldenses and Albigenses. Witness John Huss, and Jerome of Prague. Witness the Smithfield fires in England! Witness God and man against this bloody, persecuting, ruthless, and impure Church!

And think to change times and laws] Appointing fasts and feasts; canonizing persons whom he chooses to call saints; granting pardons and indulgences for sins; instituting new modes of worship utterly unknown to the Christian Church; new articles of faith; new rules of practice; and reversing, with pleasure, the laws both of God and man.–Dodd" (Emphasis his; Clarke's Commentary on the Bible, Volume IV, p. 594).

Who changed the Sabbath to Sunday?

Matthew 15:9 'BUT IN VAIN DO THEY WORSHIP ME, TEACHING AS DOCTRINES THE PRECEPTS OF MEN.'"

Mark 7:7 'BUT IN VAIN DO THEY WORSHIP ME, TEACHING AS DOCTRINES THE PRECEPTS OF MEN.'

It is very important that this verse is repeated twice. This is explained in Deuteronomy and Matthew. Both Old Testament and new.

Deuteronomy 19:15 "A single witness shall not rise up against a man on account of any iniquity or any sin which he has committed; on the evidence of two or three witnesses a matter shall be confirmed.

69

Matthew 18:16 But if he does not listen to you, take one or two more with you, so that BY THE MOUTH OF TWO OR THREE WITNESSES EVERY FACT MAY BE CONFIRMED.

You'll find further evidence in Isaiah.

Isaiah 8:20 To the law and to the testimony! If they do not speak according to this word, it is because they have no dawn.

"Prove to me from the Bible alone that I am bound to keep Sunday holy. There is no such law in the Bible. It is a law of the Catholic Church alone. The Catholic Church says, by my divine power I abolish the Sabbath day and command you to keep holy the first day of the week. And lo! The entire civilized world bows down in reverent obedience to the command of the Holy Catholic Church" (Thomas Enright, CSSR, President, Redemptorist College [Roman Catholic], Kansas City, MO, Feb. 18, 1884).

"The Pope has power to change times, to abrogate laws, and to dispense with all things, even the precepts of Christ. The Pope has authority and has often exercised it, to dispense with the command of Christ" (Decretal, de Tranlatic Episcop).

It is a matter of Biblical and secular history that God never changed His holy Sabbath or transferred its solemnity to Sunday. Who did?

The Roman government along with the Roman Catholic Church, changed Sabbath to Sunday!

Chapter 8

HOLY DAYS VS. HOLIDAYS

∞

H oly days (the seven feasts) vs. pagan holidays–Christmas, Easter, valentines day, etc.

The Truth is that Dec. 25th is not Jesus' birthday. It is the worship of the sun and not the Son! It is a pagan holiday. The Truth is that we should not be celebrating His birth, but His sacrifice. Romans celebrated birthdays.

December 25 corresponds with the Roman solar holiday *Dies Natalis Solis Invicti*. *Dies Natalis Solis Invicti* means "the birthday of the unconquered Sun." The use of the title Sol Invictus allowed several solar deities to be worshipped collectively, including *Elah-Gabal*, a Syrian sun god; *Sol*, the god of Emperor Aurelian; and *Mithras*, a soldiers' god of Persian origin. In 245 AD, the theologian *Origen of Alexandria* stated that, "only sinners (like Pharaoh and Herod)" celebrated their birthdays. In 303 AD, Christian writer Arnobius ridiculed the idea of celebrating the birthdays of gods, which suggests that Christmas was not yet a feast at this time.

God gave us 7 Holy Days to celebrate.

HOLY DAYS CALENDAR

MONTH	CHRISTIAN	DATE	HOLY DAY
NISAN	MARCH/APRIL	Nisan 14 Nisan 15-21 Nisan 16	Passover Unleavened Bread First Fruits
SIVAN	MAY/JUNE	Sivan 6	Shavuot (weeks) —-Pentecost
TISHRI	SEPT/OCT	Tishri 1 Tishri 10 Tishri 15-21	Rosh Hashannah — —- Trumpets Yom Kipper Day of Atonement Tabernacles
KISLEV	NOV/DEC	Kislev 25 Tevet 2/3	Hanukkah

Pagans gave us Christmas, Easter, and Valentine's day.
Christmas happens near the time of the winter solstice when the sun is at its lowest time. So, Christmas is celebrating the birth of the sun NOT the Son. As far as December being the time of Jesus' birth. It is wrong. The Bible says that shepherds were in the field tending their flocks. Not in December. Also, Jesus was born at the time of the first Roman census, which was has not been documented with a date, but was around the time of the Jewish feast of Tabernacles which was around September.

Easter was supposedly named after Eostre (a.k.a. Eastre). She was the Great Mother Goddess of the Saxon people in Northern Europe. derived from the ancient word for spring: "Eastre." Eostre's sacred animal was a rabbit, and a symbol of the rebirth of life in the spring-time was the egg. Nimrod is the God of fertility. Semiramis, who was both Nimrod's wife and Tammuz' mother, was worshiped as the "mother of a god" and a "fertility goddess" because she had to be extremely fertile to give birth to all the pagan incarnate gods that represented Nimrod. Where Nimrod is the "sun god", Semiramis is the "moon goddess'.

Valentine's Day is a celebration of love and lovers. The roots of Valentine's Day goes back to ancient times, when people paid honor to the Roman God of Fertility. This was known as the Feast of Lupercalia, and was celebrated even then on February 14th. Lupercus, the Roman god after which the holiday is named, was the pagan god of fertility. cupid, an essential part of Valentine's Day lore and customs, was the Roman god of love.

I judge religions on Truth. By judge, I mean whether I want to follow their teachings or not. If a religion is based on lies, then I will not follow it. They have to teach from the Bible.

In the Bible, God tells us that we are not to add or delete any-thing from the book. **Deuteronomy 4:2** You shall not add to the word which I am commanding you, nor take away from it, that you may keep the commandments of the LORD your God which I com-mand you. **Revelation 22:18-19** I testify to everyone who hears the words of the prophecy of this book: if anyone adds to them, God will add to him the plagues which are written in this book; and if anyone takes away from the words of the book of this prophecy, God will take away his part from the tree of life and from the holy city, which are written in this book.

He says to not call anyone Father except the Father. **Matthew 23:9** Do not call *anyone* on earth your father; for One is your Father, He who is in heaven. He gives us the Holy Days to follow. He gives us the day that we are to rest and worship on. He tells us not to worship Idols.

As far as easter is concerned.. Passover was the time of Jesus' resurrection, not easter. Easter is about the pagan god nimrod, the pagan god of fertility. That is why easter bunnies and easter eggs are celebrated.

The 7 Holy Days are more about Jesus. There are 7 feast days. 4 spring feasts which have been fulfilled by Christ and 3 fall feasts which are yet to be fulfilled.

Four Feasts–In the Spring
(Already Fulfilled)

Pesach–Passover:
(Jesus was our Passover Lamb)

Unleavened Bread:
(Jesus was our sinless Messiah)
First Fruits:
(Jesus was the first to be raised from the dead)

Shavuot–Pentecost:
(The Holy Spirit descended)

Three Feasts–In the Fall
(Yet to be fulfilled)

Rosh Hoshanah–Feast of Trumpets 'The Blowing of the Shofar'
(Will announce Jesus' return)

Yom Kippur–Day of Atonement
(Judgment Day)

Succot–Feast of Tabernacles
(The Kingdom banquet)

HOLY DAYS – BIBLICAL FEASTS

**The first 4 have been fulfilled – the last 3 are yet to be fulfilled.
The first 4 were fulfilled on the exact dates!
What does that say about the last 3?**

Leviticus 23:1-4–Laws of Religious Festivals

The LORD spoke again to Moses, saying, [2] "Speak to the sons of Israel and say to them, 'The LORD's appointed times which you shall proclaim as holy convocations—My appointed times are these: [3] 'For six days work may be done, but on the seventh day there is a Sabbath of complete rest, a holy convocation. You shall not do any work; it is a Sabbath to the LORD in all your dwellings. [4] 'These are the appointed times of the LORD, holy convocations which you shall proclaim at the times appointed for them.

PASSOVER – The first Feast of the Lord is Passover–Christ our Passover has been sacrificed. Passover occurs in the spring of the year, on the fourteenth day of the Hebrew month, Nisan (March/April).

Leviticus 23:5 In the first month, on the fourteenth day of the month at twilight is the Lord's Passover. God told Moses that He had seen the affliction of His people in Egypt. He heard their cry for help and He knew their sorrows. He was coming to deliver the out of Egyptian bondage an to bring them into the promised land.

UNLEAVENED BREAD – Clean out old leaven…just as you are in fact unleavened. Leviticus 23:6-8 Then on the fifteenth day of the same month there is the Feast of Unleavened Bread to the Lord; for seven days you shall eat unleavened bread. On the first day you shall have a holy convocation; you shall not do any laborious work. But for seven days you shall present an offering by fire to the Lord. On the seventh day is a holy convocation; you shall not do any laborious work.'"

Exodus 12:14–Feast of Unleavened Bread–[14] 'Now this day will be a memorial to you, and you shall celebrate it *as* a feast to the Lord; throughout your generations you are to celebrate it *as* a permanent ordinance. In the Bible, leaven symbolizes error or evil.

Exodus 12:17 You shall also observe the *Feast of* Unleavened Bread, for on this very day I brought your hosts out of the land of Egypt; therefore you shall observe this day throughout your generations as a permanent ordinance.

1 Corinthians 5:7-8–[7] Clean out the old leaven so that you may be a new lump, just as you are *in fact* unleavened. For Christ our Passover also has been sacrificed. [8] Therefore let us celebrate the feast, not with old leaven, nor with the leaven of malice and wickedness, but with the unleavened bread of sincerity and truth.

The Messiah was crucified on Passover. He was taken from the cross and placed in a borrowed tomb. Unlike other corpses, His body would not decay in the grave. There would be no decomposition of His flesh. His body would be exempted from the divine pronouncement that from the dust of the ground man came and to the dust of he shall return. **Genesis 3:19** By the sweat of your face You will eat bread, Till you return to the ground, Because from it you were taken; For you are dust, And to dust you shall return." This should not catch us off guard because Christ allowed us to listen in on a conversation He had with the Father–**Acts 2:27** BECAUSE YOU WILL NOT ABANDON MY SOUL TO HADES, NOR ALLOW YOUR HOLY ONE TO UNDERGO DECAY. **Psalm 16:10–**For You will not abandon my soul to Sheol; Nor will You allow Your Holy One to undergo decay.

The third feast occurs on th second day of the seven-day Feast of Unleavened Bread. It is called the Feast of Firstfruits. Passover occurs on the fourteenth of Nisan; the first day of the Feast of Unleavened Bread occurs on the fifteenth; and Firstfruits occurs on the sixteenth day of Nisan.

FIRST FRUITS – Christ has been raised – the first fruits!

Leviticus 23:9 10, 14–⁹Then the LORD spoke to Moses, saying, ¹⁰ "Speak to the sons of Israel and say to them, 'When you enter the land which I am going to give to you and reap its harvest, then you shall bring in the sheaf of the first fruits of your harvest to the priest. ¹⁴Until this same day, until you have brought in the offering of your God, you shall eat neither bread nor roasted grain nor new growth. It is to be a perpetual statute throughout your generations in all your dwelling places.

In both the Old and New Testaments, there were people who were raised from the dead. In time, however they died again. **Jesus was**

the first to be resurrected fro the grave, never to die again. He alone is the Firstfruits.

some examples of people who were raised from the dead

1 Kings 17:17-23–Elijah Raises the Widow's Son

[17] Now it came about after these things that the son of the woman, the mistress of the house, became sick; and his sickness was so severe that there was no breath left in him. [18] So she said to Elijah, "What do I have to do with you, O man of God? You have come to me to bring my iniquity to remembrance and to put my son to death!" [19] He said to her, "Give me your son." Then he took him from her bosom and carried him up to the upper room where he was living, and laid him on his own bed. [20] He called to the LORD and said, "O LORD my God, have You also brought calamity to the widow with whom I am staying, by causing her son to die?" [21] Then he stretched himself upon the child three times, and called to the LORD and said, "O LORD my God, I pray You, let this child's life return to him." [22] The LORD heard the voice of Elijah, and the life of the child returned to him and he revived. [23] Elijah took the child and brought him down from the upper room into the house and gave him to his mother; and Elijah said, "See, your son is alive."

2 Kings 4:18-37–The Shunammite's Son

[18] When the child was grown, the day came that he went out to his father to the reapers. [19] He said to his father, "My head, my head." And he said to his servant, "Carry him to his mother." [20] When he had taken him and brought him to his mother, he sat on her lap until noon, and *then* died. [21] She went up and laid him on the bed of the man of God, and shut *the door* behind him and went out. [22] Then she called to her husband and said, "Please send me one of

the servants and one of the donkeys, that I may run to the man of God and return." ²³ He said, "Why will you go to him today? It is neither new moon nor sabbath." And she said, "*It will be* well." ²⁴ Then she saddled a donkey and said to her servant, "Drive and go forward; do not slow down the pace for me unless I tell you." ²⁵ So she went and came to the man of God to Mount Carmel.

When the man of God saw her at a distance, he said to Gehazi his servant, "Behold, there is the Shunammite. ²⁶ Please run now to meet her and say to her, 'Is it well with you? Is it well with your husband? Is it well with the child?'" And she answered, "It is well." ²⁷ When she came to the man of God to the hill, she caught hold of his feet. And Gehazi came near to push her away; but the man of God said, "Let her alone, for her soul is troubled within her; and the LORD has hidden it from me and has not told me." ²⁸ Then she said, "Did I ask for a son from my lord? Did I not say, 'Do not deceive me'?"

²⁹ Then he said to Gehazi, "Gird up your loins and take my staff in your hand, and go your way; if you meet any man, do not salute him, and if anyone salutes you, do not answer him; and lay my staff on the lad's face." ³⁰ The mother of the lad said, "As the LORD lives and as you yourself live, I will not leave you." And he arose and followed her. ³¹ Then Gehazi passed on before them and laid the staff on the lad's face, but there was no sound or response. So he returned to meet him and told him, "The lad has not awakened."

³² When Elisha came into the house, behold the lad was dead and laid on his bed. ³³ So he entered and shut the door behind them both and prayed to the LORD. ³⁴ And he went up and lay on the child, and put his mouth on his mouth and his eyes on his eyes and his hands on his hands, and he stretched himself on him; and the flesh of the child became warm. ³⁵ Then he returned and walked in the house

once back and forth, and went up and stretched himself on him; and the lad sneezed seven times and the lad opened his eyes. [36] He called Gehazi and said, "Call this Shunammite." So he called her. And when she came in to him, he said, "Take up your son." [37] Then she went in and fell at his feet and bowed herself to the ground, and she took up her son and went out.

Luke 8:54-55– [54] He, however, took her by the hand and called, saying, "Child, arise!" [55] And her spirit returned, and she got up immediately; and He gave orders for something to be given her to eat.

John 11:43-44– [43] When He had said these things, He cried out with a loud voice, "Lazarus, come forth." [44] The man who had died came forth, bound hand and foot with wrappings, and his face was wrapped around with a cloth. Jesus *said to them, "Unbind him, and let him go."

The Passover spoke of Christ's death as a sacrificial substitutionary lamb

The feast of Unleavened bread indicated that His body would not decay in the grave.

The Feast of Firstfruits proclaims that death could not hold Him

1 Corinthians 15:20-23–The Order of Resurrection [20] But now Christ has been raised from the dead, the first fruits of those who are asleep. [21] For since by a man *came* death, by a man also *came* the resurrection of the dead. [22] For as in Adam all die, so also in Christ all will be made alive. [23] But each in his own order: Christ the first fruits, after that those who are Christ's at His coming,

PENTECOST OR FEAST OF WEEKS or Shavuot – promise of the Spirit, mystery of the church; Jews-Gentiles in one body. The outpouring of the spirit.

John 16:7–But I tell you the truth, it is to your advantage that I go away; for if I do not go away, the Helper will not come to you; but if I go, I will send Him to you.

Acts 1:9–The Ascension–And after He had said these things, He was lifted up while they were looking on, and a cloud received Him out of their sight.

Leviticus 23:15, 16, 21, 22 [15] 'You shall also count for yourselves from the day after the Sabbath, from the day when you brought in the sheaf of the wave offering; there shall be seven complete Sabbaths. [16] You shall count fifty days to the day after the seventh Sabbath; then you shall present a new grain offering to the LORD. [21] On this same day you shall make a proclamation as well; you are to have a holy convocation. You shall do no laborious work. **It is to be a perpetual statute in all your dwelling places throughout your generations.** [22] 'When you reap the harvest of your land, moreover, you shall not reap to the very corners of your field nor gather the gleaning of your harvest; you are to leave them for the needy and the alien. I am the LORD your God.'"

Acts 2:1–The Day of Pentecost- When the day of Pentecost had come, they were all together in one place.

Ephesians 2:18, 22–[18] for through Him we both have our access in one Spirit to the Father. [22] in whom you also are being built together into a dwelling of God in the Spirit.

The Three Fall Feasts which are yet to be fulfilled. They predict with certainty, events that will yet unfold. As the four spring holidays were fulfilled literally and right on schedule in connection with Christ's first coming, the three fall Holy Days will likely be fulfilled literally and right on schedule with His second coming.

FEAST OF TRUMPETS – the gathering in preparation for the final day of atonement. The Feast of Trumpets is the first of the fall feasts. It is called Rosh Hashana by the Jewish people, which literally means Head of the Year.

Ephesians 2:18-22–[18] for through Him we both have our access in one Spirit to the Father. [19] So then you are no longer strangers and aliens, but you are fellow citizens with the saints, and are of God's household, [20] having been built on the foundation of the apostles and prophets, Christ Jesus Himself being the corner *stone*, [21] in whom the whole building, being fitted together, is growing into a holy temple in the Lord, [22] in whom you also are being built together into a dwelling of God in the Spirit.

Numbers 29:1–'Now in the seventh month, on the first day of the month, you shall also have a holy convocation; you shall do no laborious work. It will be to you a day for blowing trumpets.

1 Thessalonians 4:13-18–Those Who Died in Christ [13] But we do not want you to be uninformed, brethren, about those who are asleep, so that you will not grieve as do the rest who have no hope. [14] For if we believe that Jesus died and rose again, even so God will bring with Him those who have fallen asleep in Jesus. [15] For this we say to you by the word of the Lord, that we who are alive and remain until the coming of the Lord, will not precede those who have fallen asleep. [16] For the Lord Himself will descend from heaven with a shout, with the voice of *the* archangel and **with the**

trumpet of God, and the dead in Christ will rise first. [17] Then we who are alive and remain will be caught up together with them in the clouds to meet the Lord in the air, and so we shall always be with the Lord. [18] Therefore comfort one another with these words.

DAY OF ATONEMENT – all will look to one Messiah in one day

Leviticus 16:30-31– [30] for it is on this day that atonement shall be made for you to cleanse you; you will be clean from all your sins before the LORD. [31] It is to be a Sabbath of solemn rest for you, that you may humble your souls; **it is a permanent statute.**

Leviticus 23:26-32–The Day of Atonement

[26] The LORD spoke to Moses, saying, [27] "On exactly the tenth day of this seventh month is the day of atonement; it shall be a holy convocation for you, and you shall humble your souls and present an offering by fire to the LORD. [28] You shall not do any work on this same day, for it is a day of atonement, to make atonement on your behalf before the LORD your God. [29] If there is any person who will not humble himself on this same day, he shall be cut off from his people. [30] As for any person who does any work on this same day, that person I will destroy from among his people. [31] **You shall do no work at all. It is to be a perpetual statute throughout your generations in all your dwelling places. [32] It is to be a Sabbath of complete rest to you, and you shall humble your souls; on the ninth of the month at evening, from evening until evening you shall keep your Sabbath."**

Numbers 29:7– 'Then on the tenth day of this seventh month you shall have a holy convocation, and you shall humble yourselves; you shall not do any work.

Zechariah 12:10 "I will pour out on the house of David and on the inhabitants of Jerusalem, the Spirit of grace and of supplication, so that they will look on Me whom they have pierced; and they will mourn for Him, as one mourns for an only son, and they will weep bitterly over Him like the bitter weeping over a firstborn.

Romans 11:25-29– [25] For I do not want you, brethren, to be uninformed of this mystery—so that you will not be wise in your own estimation—that a partial hardening has happened to Israel until the fullness of the Gentiles has come in; [26] and so all Israel will be saved; just as it is written,

"THE DELIVERER WILL COME FROM ZION,
HE WILL REMOVE UNGODLINESS FROM JACOB."
[27] "THIS IS MY COVENANT WITH THEM,
WHEN I TAKE AWAY THEIR SINS."

[28] From the standpoint of the gospel they are enemies for your sake, but from the standpoint of *God's* choice they are beloved for the sake of the fathers; [29] for the gifts and the calling of God are irrevocable.

Hebrews 7:27– who does not need daily, like those high priests, to offer up sacrifices, first for His own sins and then for the *sins* of the people, because this He did once for all when He offered up Himself.

Hebrews 9:12 and not through the blood of goats and calves, but through His own blood, He entered the holy place once for all, having obtained eternal redemption.

Hebrews 10:10 By this will we have been sanctified through the offering of the body of Jesus Christ once for all.

FEAST OF TABERNACLES – families will gather to celebrate the Feast of Booths

Leviticus 23:33-44 [33] Again the LORD spoke to Moses, saying, [34] "Speak to the sons of Israel, saying, 'On the fifteenth of this seventh month is the Feast of Booths for seven days to the LORD. [35] On the first day is a holy convocation; you shall do no laborious work of any kind. [36] For seven days you shall present an offering by fire to the LORD. On the eighth day you shall have a holy convocation and present an offering by fire to the LORD; it is an assembly. You shall do no laborious work.

[37] 'These are the appointed times of the LORD which you shall proclaim as holy convocations, to present offerings by fire to the LORD— burnt offerings and grain offerings, sacrifices and drink offerings, *each* day's matter on its own day— [38] besides *those of* the Sabbaths of the LORD, and besides your gifts and besides all your votive and freewill offerings, which you give to the LORD.

[39] 'On exactly the fifteenth day of the seventh month, when you have gathered in the crops of the land, you shall celebrate the feast of the LORD for seven days, with a rest on the first day and a rest on the eighth day. [40] Now on the first day you shall take for yourselves the foliage of beautiful trees, palm branches and boughs of leafy trees and willows of the brook, and you shall rejoice before the LORD your God for seven days. [41] You shall thus celebrate it *as* a feast to the LORD for seven days in the year. **It *shall be* a perpetual statute throughout your generations;** you shall celebrate it in the seventh month. [42] You shall live in booths for seven days;

85

all the native-born in Israel shall live in booths, [43] so that your generations may know that I had the sons of Israel live in booths when I brought them out from the land of Egypt. I am the LORD your God.'" [44] So Moses declared to the sons of Israel the appointed times of the LORD.

Numbers 29:12– 'Then on the fifteenth day of the seventh month you shall have a holy convocation; you shall do no laborious work, and you shall observe a feast to the LORD for seven days.

Zechariah 14:16-19– [16] Then it will come about that any who are left of all the nations that went against Jerusalem will go up from year to year to worship the King, the LORD of hosts, and to celebrate the Feast of Booths. [17] And it will be that whichever of the families of the earth does not go up to Jerusalem to worship the King, the LORD of hosts, there will be no rain on them. [18] If the family of Egypt does not go up or enter, then no *rain will fall* on them; it will be the plague with which the LORD smites the nations who do not go up to celebrate the Feast of Booths. [19] This will be the punishment of Egypt, and the punishment of all the nations who do not go up to celebrate the Feast of Booths.

HOLY DAYS/DATES CALENDAR

Roman Year	New Testament Passover (at sundown)	Feast of Unleavened Bread	Feast of Pentecost	Feast of Trumpets
2019	April 18	April 20-26	June 9	September 30
2020	April 7	April 9-15	May 31	September 19
2021	March 26	March 28 – April 3	May 16	September 26
2022	April 14	April 16-22	June 5	September 26

Roman Year	Day of Atonement	Feast of Tabernacles	Last Great Day
2019	October 9	October 14-20	October 21
2020	September 28	October 3-9	October 10
2021	September 16	September 21-27	September 28
2022	October 5	October 10-16	October 17

The Jewish Calendar			
MONTH	**LENGTH**	**DATE**	**HOLIDAY**
Nisan	30 days	Nisan 14 Nisan 15-21 Nisan 16	Passover Unlevened Bread Firstfruits
Sivan	30 days	Sivan 6	Shavuot (weeks) Pentecost
Av	30 days	Av 9	Tish B' Av
Tishri	30 days	Tishri 1 Tishri 10 Tishri 15-21	Rosh Hashannah–trumpets Yom Kipper–Atonement Tabernacles
Kislev	29 or 30 days	Kislev 25 Tevet 2/3	Hanukkah
Adar	29 days 30 in leap year	Adar 14	Purim–feast of Esther

Chapter 9

WHAT ARE THE COVENANTS IN THE BIBLE?

∾

The Bible speaks of seven different covenants, four of which (Abrahamic, Palestinian, Mosaic, Davidic) God made with the nation of Israel. Of those four, three are unconditional in nature; that is, regardless of Israel's obedience or disobedience, God still will fulfill these covenants with Israel. One of the covenants, the Mosaic Covenant, is conditional in nature. That is, this covenant will bring either blessing or cursing depending on Israel's obedience or disobedience. Three of the covenants (Adamic, Noahic, New) are made between God and mankind in general, and are not limited to the nation of Israel.

The **Adamic Covenant** can be thought of in two parts: the Edenic Covenant (innocence) and the Adamic Covenant (grace).

The **Edenic Covenant** is found in **Genesis 1:26-30**; ²⁶Then God said, "Let Us make man in Our image, according to Our likeness; and let them rule over the fish of the sea and over the birds of the sky and over the cattle and over all the earth, and over every creeping thing that creeps on the earth." ²⁷God created man in His own image, in the image of God He created him; male and female He created them. [28] God blessed them; and God said to them, "Be fruitful and multiply, and fill the earth, and subdue it; and rule over the fish of the sea and over the birds of the sky and over every living thing that moves on the earth." [29] Then God said, "Behold, I have given you every plant yielding seed that is on the surface of all the earth, and every tree which has fruit yielding seed; it shall be food for you; [30] and to every beast of the earth and to every bird of the sky and to every thing that moves on the earth which has life, *I have given* every green plant for food"; and it was so. and **Genesis 2:16-17**. [16] The LORD God commanded the man, saying, "From any tree of the garden you may eat freely; [17] but from the tree of the knowledge of good and evil you shall not eat, for in the day that you eat from it you will surely die."

The **Edenic Covenant** outlined man's responsibility toward creation and God's directive regarding the tree of the knowledge of good and evil.

The **Adamic Covenant** included the curses pronounced against mankind for the sin of Adam and Eve, as well as God's provision for that sin **Genesis 3:15-19** And I will put enmity Between you and the woman, And between your seed and her seed; He shall bruise you on the head, And you shall bruise him on the heel." [16] To the woman He said, "I will greatly multiply Your pain in childbirth, In pain you will bring forth children; Yet your desire will be for your husband, And he will rule over you." [17] Then to Adam He said, "Because you have listened to the voice of your wife, and have eaten from the tree about which I commanded you, saying, 'You shall not eat from it'; Cursed is the ground because of you;

In toil you will eat of it All the days of your life. [18] "Both thorns and thistles it shall grow for you; And you will eat the plants of the field; [19] By the sweat of your face You will eat bread, Till you return to the ground, Because from it you were taken; For you are dust, And to dust you shall return."

The **Noahic Covenant** was an unconditional covenant between God and Noah (specifically) and humanity (generally). After the Flood, God promised humanity that He would never again destroy all life on earth with a Flood (see Genesis chapter 9). God gave the rainbow as the sign of the covenant, a promise that the entire earth would never again flood and a reminder that God can and will judge sin **2 Peter 2:5** [5] and did not spare the ancient world, but preserved Noah, a preacher of righteousness, with seven others, when He brought a flood upon the world of the ungodly;

Abrahamic Covenant–Genesis 12:1-7; Now the LORD said to Abram, "Go forth from your country,

And from your relatives And from your father's house, To the land which I will show you; [2] And I will make you a great nation, And I will bless you, And make your name great; And so you shall be a blessing;

[3] And I will bless those who bless you, And the one who curses you I will curse. And in you all the families of the earth will be blessed."

[4] So Abram went forth as the LORD had spoken to him; and Lot went with him. Now Abram was seventy-five years old when he departed from Haran. [5] Abram took Sarai his wife and Lot his nephew, and all their possessions which they had accumulated, and the persons which they had acquired in Haran, and they set out for the land of Canaan; thus they came to the land of Canaan. [6] Abram passed through the land as far as the site of Shechem, to the oak of Moreh. Now the Canaanite *was* then in the land. [7] The LORD appeared to

Abram and said, "To your descendants I will give this land." So he built an altar there to the LORD who had appeared to him.

Genesis 13:14-17 [14] The LORD said to Abram, after Lot had separated from him, "Now lift up your eyes and look from the place where you are, northward and southward and eastward and westward; [15] for all the land which you see, I will give it to you and to your descendants forever. [16] I will make your descendants as the dust of the earth, so that if anyone can number the dust of the earth, then your descendants can also be numbered. [17] Arise, walk about the land through its length and breadth; for I will give it to you."

Genesis 15; After these things the word of the LORD came to Abram in a vision, saying,

"Do not fear, Abram, I am a shield to you; Your reward shall be very great."

[2] Abram said, "O Lord GOD, what will You give me, since I am childless, and the heir of my house is Eliezer of Damascus?" [3] And Abram said, "Since You have given no offspring to me, one born in my house is my heir." [4] Then behold, the word of the LORD came to him, saying, "This man will not be your heir; but one who will come forth from your own body, he shall be your heir." [5] And He took him outside and said, "Now look toward the heavens, and count the stars, if you are able to count them." And He said to him, "So shall your descendants be." [6] Then he believed in the LORD; and He reckoned it to him as righteousness. [7] And He said to him, "I am the LORD who brought you out of Ur of the Chaldeans, to give you this land to possess it." [8] He said, "O Lord GOD, how may I know that I will possess it?" [9] So He said to him, "Bring Me a three year old heifer, and a three year old female goat, and a three year old ram, and a turtledove, and a young pigeon." [10] Then he brought all

these to Him and cut them in two, and laid each half opposite the other; but he did not cut the birds. [11] The birds of prey came down upon the carcasses, and Abram drove them away.

[12] Now when the sun was going down, a deep sleep fell upon Abram; and behold, terror *and* great darkness fell upon him. [13] *God* said to Abram, "Know for certain that your descendants will be strangers in a land that is not theirs, where they will be enslaved and oppressed four hundred years. [14] But I will also judge the nation whom they will serve, and afterward they will come out with many possessions. [15] As for you, you shall go to your fathers in peace; you will be buried at a good old age. [16] Then in the fourth generation they will return here, for the iniquity of the Amorite is not yet complete."

[17] It came about when the sun had set, that it was very dark, and behold, *there appeared* a smoking oven and a flaming torch which passed between these pieces. [18] On that day the LORD made a covenant with Abram, saying, "To your descendants I have given this land, From the river of Egypt as far as the great river, the river Euphrates: [19] the Kenite and the Kenizzite and the Kadmonite [20] and the Hittite and the Perizzite and the Rephaim [21] and the Amorite and the Canaanite and the Girgashite and the Jebusite."

Genesis 17:1-14 Now when Abram was ninety-nine years old, the LORD appeared to Abram and said to him,

"I am God Almighty;
Walk before Me, and be blameless.
[2] "I will establish My covenant between Me and you,
And I will multiply you exceedingly."

[3] Abram fell on his face, and God talked with him, saying,

[4] "As for Me, behold, My covenant is with you,
And you will be the father of a multitude of nations.
[5] "No longer shall your name be called Abram,
But your name shall be Abraham;
For I have made you the father of a multitude of nations.

[6] I will make you exceedingly fruitful, and I will make nations of you, and kings will come forth from you. [7] I will establish My covenant between Me and you and your descendants after you throughout their generations for an everlasting covenant, to be God to you and to your descendants after you. [8] I will give to you and to your descendants after you, the land of your sojournings, all the land of Canaan, for an everlasting possession; and I will be their God."

[9] God said further to Abraham, "Now as for you, you shall keep My covenant, you and your descendants after you throughout their generations. [10] This is My covenant, which you shall keep, between Me and you and your descendants after you: every male among you shall be circumcised. [11] And you shall be circumcised in the flesh of your foreskin, and it shall be the sign of the covenant between Me and you. [12] And every male among you who is eight days old shall be circumcised throughout your generations, a *servant* who is born in the house or who is bought with money from any foreigner, who is not of your descendants. [13] A *servant* who is born in your house or who is bought with your money shall surely be circumcised; thus shall My covenant be in your flesh for an everlasting covenant. [14] But an uncircumcised male who is not circumcised in the flesh of his foreskin, that person shall be cut off from his people; he has broken My covenant."

Genesis 22:15-18 [15] Then the angel of the LORD called to Abraham a second time from heaven, [16] and said, "By Myself I have sworn, declares the LORD, because you have done this thing and have not withheld your son, your only son, [17] indeed I will greatly bless you, and I will greatly multiply your seed as the stars of the heavens and as the sand which is on the seashore; and your seed shall possess the gate of their enemies. [18] In your seed all the nations of the earth shall be blessed, because you have obeyed My voice."

In this covenant, God promised many things to Abraham. He personally promised that He would make Abraham's name great (Genesis 12:2), that Abraham would have numerous physical descendants (Genesis 13:16), and that he would be the father of a multitude of nations (Genesis 17:4-5). God also made promises regarding a nation called Israel. In fact, the geographical boundaries of the Abrahamic Covenant are laid out on more than one occasion in the book of Genesis. Another provision in the Abrahamic Covenant is that the families of the world will be blessed through the physical line of Abraham. This is a reference to the Messiah, who would come from the line of Abraham.

Palestinian Covenant (Deuteronomy 30:1-10). "So it shall be when all of these things have come upon you, the blessing and the curse which I have set before you, and you call *them* to mind in all nations where the LORD your God has banished you, [2] and you return to the LORD your God and obey Him with all your heart and soul according to all that I command you today, you and your sons, [3] then the LORD your God will restore you from captivity, and have compassion on you, and will gather you again from all the peoples where the LORD your God has scattered you. [4] If your outcasts are at the ends of the earth, from there the LORD your God will gather you, and from there He will bring you back. [5] The LORD your God will bring you into the land which your fathers possessed, and you shall possess it; and He will prosper you and multiply you more than your fathers.

⁶ "Moreover the LORD your God will circumcise your heart and the heart of your descendants, to love the LORD your God with all your heart and with all your soul, so that you may live. ⁷ The LORD your God will inflict all these curses on your enemies and on those who hate you, who persecuted you. ⁸ And you shall again obey the LORD, and observe all His commandments which I command you today. ⁹ Then the LORD your God will prosper you abundantly in all the work of your hand, in the offspring of your body and in the ᶠoffspring of your cattle and in the produce of your ground, for the LORD will again rejoice over you for good, just as He rejoiced over your fathers; ¹⁰ if you obey the LORD your God to keep His commandments and His statutes which are written in this book of the law, if you turn to the LORD your God with all your heart and soul.

The Palestinian Covenant, or Land Covenant, amplifies the land aspect that was detailed in the Abrahamic Covenant. According to the terms of this covenant, if the people disobeyed, God would cause them to be scattered around the world (**Deuteronomy 30:3-4**), but He would eventually restore the nation (**verse 5**). When the nation is restored, then they will obey Him perfectly (verse 8), and God will cause them to prosper (**verse 9**).

Mosaic Covenant (Deuteronomy 11). The Mosaic Covenant was a conditional covenant that either brought God's direct blessing for obedience or God's direct cursing for disobedience upon the nation of Israel. Part of the Mosaic Covenant was the Ten Commandments (**Exodus 20**) and the rest of the Law, which contained over 600 commands—roughly 300 positive and 300 negative. The history books of the Old Testament (Joshua–Esther) detail how Israel succeeded at obeying the Law or how Israel failed miserably at obeying the Law. **Deuteronomy 11:26-28** details the blessing/curse. ²⁶ "See, I am setting before you today a blessing and a curse: ²⁷ the blessing, if you listen to the commandments of the LORD your God, which I am commanding you today; [28] and the curse, if you do not listen to the commandments of the LORD your God, but turn aside from the way which I am commanding you today, by following other gods which you have not known.

Davidic Covenant (2 Samuel 7:8-16). [8] "Now therefore, thus you shall say to My servant David, 'Thus says the LORD of hosts, "I took you from the pasture, from following the sheep, to be ruler over My people Israel. [9] I have been with you wherever you have gone and have cut off all your enemies from before you; and I will make you a great name, like the names of the great men who are on the earth. [10] I will also appoint a place for My people Israel and will plant them, that they may live in their own place and not be disturbed again, nor will the wicked afflict them any more as formerly, [11] even from the day that I commanded judges to be over My people Israel; and I will give you rest from all your enemies. The LORD also declares to you that the LORD will make a house for you. [12] When your days are complete and you lie down with your fathers, I will raise up your descendant after you, who will come forth from you, and I will establish his kingdom. [13] He shall build a house for My name, and I will establish the throne of his kingdom forever. [14] I will be a father to him and he will be a son to Me; when he commits iniquity, I will correct him with the rod of men and the strokes of the sons of men, [15] but My lovingkindness shall not depart from him, as I took *it* away from Saul, whom I removed from before you. [16] Your house and your kingdom shall endure before Me forever; your throne shall be established forever."'"

The Davidic Covenant amplifies the "seed" aspect of the Abrahamic Covenant. The promises to David in this passage are significant. God promised that David's lineage would last forever and that his kingdom would never pass away permanently (verse 16). Obviously, the Davidic throne has not been in place at all times.

There will be a time, however, when someone from the line of David will again sit on the throne and rule as king. This future king is Jesus (Luke 1:32-33). [32] He will be great and will be called the Son of the Most High; and the Lord God will give Him the throne of His father David; [33] and He will reign over the house of Jacob forever, and His kingdom will have no end."

New Covenant (Jeremiah 31:31-34). [31] "Behold, days are coming," declares the LORD, "when I will make a new covenant with the house of Israel and with the house of Judah, [32] not like the covenant which I made with their fathers in the day I took them by the hand to bring them out of the land of Egypt, My covenant which they broke, although I was a husband to them," declares the LORD. [33] "But this is the covenant which I will make with the house of Israel after those days," declares the LORD, "I will put My law within them and on their heart I will write it; and I will be their God, and they shall be My people. [34] They will not teach again, each man his neighbor and each man his brother, saying, 'Know the LORD,' for they will all know Me, from the least of them to the greatest of them," declares the LORD, "for I will forgive their iniquity, and their sin I will remember no more."

The New Covenant is a covenant made first with the nation of Israel and, ultimately, with all mankind.

In the New Covenant, God promises to forgive sin, and there will be a universal knowledge of the Lord. Jesus Christ came to fulfill the Law of Moses **Matthew 5:17** [17] "Do not think that I came to abolish the Law or the Prophets; I did not come to abolish but to fulfill.) and create a new covenant between God and His people. Now that we are under the New Covenant, both Jews and Gentiles can be free from the penalty of the Law. We are now given the opportunity to receive salvation as a free gift (**Ephesians 2:8-9**)

[8] For by grace you have been saved through faith; and that not of yourselves, *it is* the gift of God; [9] not as a result of works, so that no one may boast.

To me the most important thing to remember is that even though there are new covenants, God's word does not change. Each covenant was given for a reason and each reason is valid for us today. Like when Jesus came. He brought Love. Love was always there, but Jesus (Yeshua) gave meaning to love.

Paul expressed it best in **1 Corinthians 13**–If I speak with the tongues of men and of angels, but do not have love, I have become a noisy gong or a clanging cymbal. [2] If I have *the gift of* prophecy, and know all mysteries and all knowledge; and if I have all faith, so as to remove mountains, but do not have love, I am nothing. [3] And if I give all my possessions to feed *the poor*, and if I surrender my body to be burned, but do not have love, it profits me nothing.

[4] Love is patient, love is kind *and* is not jealous; love does not brag *and* is not arrogant, [5] does not act unbecomingly; it does not seek its own, is not provoked, does not take into account a wrong *suffered*, [6] does not rejoice in unrighteousness, but rejoices with the truth; [7] bears all things, believes all things, hopes all things, endures all things.

[8] Love never fails; but if *there are gifts of* prophecy, they will be done away; if *there are* tongues, they will cease; if *there is* knowledge, it will be done away. [9] For we know in part and we prophesy in part; [10] but when the perfect comes, the partial will be done away. [11] When I was a child, I used to speak like a child, think like a child, reason like a child; when I became a man, I did away with childish things. [12] For now we see in a mirror dimly, but then face to face; now I know in part, but then I will know fully just as I also have

been fully known. [13] But now faith, hope, love, abide these three; but the greatest of these is love.

1 Peter 4:10

[10] As each one has received a *special* gift, employ it in serving one another as good stewards of the manifold grace of God.

"There Is Nothing New Under The Sun"
Ecclesiastes 1:4-11

A generation goes, and a generation comes,
but the earth remains forever.

The sun rises, and the sun goes down,
and hastens to the place where it rises.

The wind blows to the south
and goes around to the north;
around and around goes the wind,
and on its circuits the wind returns.

All streams run to the sea,
but the sea is not full;
to the place where the streams flow,
there they flow again.

All things are full of weariness;
a man cannot utter it;
the eye is not satisfied with seeing,
nor the ear filled with hearing.

What has been is what will be,
and what has been done is what will be done,
and there is nothing new under the sun.

Is there a thing of which it is said,
"See, this is new"?
It has been already
in the ages before us.

There is no remembrance of former things,
nor will there be any remembrance
of later things yet to be among those who come after.

Chapter 10

THE LAW

∽

Acts 4:10-12–[10] let it be known to all of you and to all the people of Israel, that by the name of Jesus Christ the Nazarene, whom you crucified, whom God raised from the dead — by this *name* this man stands here before you in good health. [11] He is the STONE WHICH WAS REJECTED by you, THE BUILDERS, *but* WHICH BECAME THE CHIEF CORNER *stone*. [12] And there is salvation in no one else; for there is no other name under heaven that has been given among men by which we must be saved."

Jesus is the most powerful name in the whole universe. Salvation only comes through one person–Jesus. **Matthew 1:21**–She will bear a Son; and you shall call His name Jesus, for He will save His people from their sins."

1 Corinthians 1:23-24–[23] but we preach Christ crucified, to Jews a stumbling block and to Gentiles foolishness, [24] but to those who are the called, both Jews and Greeks, Christ the power of God and the wisdom of God.

Jesus is referred to as "the power of God"

1 Peter 1:13–Therefore, prepare your minds for action, keep sober *in spirit*, fix your hope completely on the grace to be brought to you at the revelation of Jesus Christ.

Grace brought to you by Jesus is "The Power of God"

Ephesians 2:8–For by grace you have been saved through faith; and that not of yourselves, *it is* the gift of God;

1 Peter 1:3-5–[3] Blessed be the God and Father of our Lord Jesus Christ, who according to His great mercy has caused us to be born again to a living hope through the resurrection of Jesus Christ from the dead, [4] to *obtain* an inheritance *which is* imperishable and undefiled and will not fade away, reserved in heaven for you, [5] who are protected by the power of God through faith for a salvation ready to be revealed in the last time.

Jesus is the only way you can be saved. Romans 1:16–For I am not ashamed of the gospel, for it is the power of God for salvation to everyone who believes, to the Jew first and also to the Greek.

Titus 2:11–For the grace of God has appeared, bringing salvation to all men,

1 John 3:4–Everyone who practices sin also practices lawlessness; and sin is lawlessness.

Sin is the transgression of the law

Romans 7:7-12–[7] What shall we say then? Is the Law sin? May it never be! On the contrary, I would not have come to know sin except through the Law; for I would not have known about coveting if the Law had not said, "YOU SHALL NOT COVET." [8] But sin, taking opportunity through the commandment, produced in me coveting of every kind; for apart from the Law sin *is* dead. [9] I was once alive apart from the Law; but when the commandment came, sin became alive and I died; [10] and this commandment, which was to result in life, proved to result in death for me; [11] for sin, taking an opportunity through the commandment, deceived me and through it killed me. [12] So then, the Law is holy, and the commandment is holy and righteous and good.

The law, the 10 commandments are found in two places, Exodus 20:1-17 and Deuteronomy 5:6-21. These are the 10 commandments that were written by God on Stone. Was this when the 10 commandments were established? God had established his laws much earlier.

Genesis 26:4-5–[4] I will multiply your descendants as the stars of heaven, and will give your descendants all these lands; and by your descendants all the nations of the earth shall be blessed; [5] because <u>Abraham obeyed Me and kept My charge, My commandments, My statutes and My laws."</u>

Even though they hadn't been written yet Abraham understood God's laws. It is easy to understand that God established his laws before The garden. What sin does is separates you from God.

Isaiah 59:1-3–Separation from God–Behold, the LORD's hand is not so short That it cannot save; Nor is His ear so dull That it cannot hear. [2] But your iniquities have made a separation between you and your God, And your sins have hidden *His* face from you so that He does not hear. [3] For your hands are defiled with blood And your fingers with iniquity; Your lips have spoken falsehood, Your tongue mutters wickedness.

Revelation 12:17–So the dragon was enraged with the woman, and went off to make war with the rest of her children, who keep the commandments of God and hold to the testimony of Jesus. The dragon is satan and the woman is the church. This verse shows that satan is angry with God's people who keep the 10 commandments and their faith in Jesus.

Some people think that Jesus did away with the law, but that is far from the truth.

Matthew 5:17-18–[17] "Do not think that I came to abolish the Law or the Prophets; I did not come to abolish but to fulfill. [18] For truly I say to you, until heaven and earth pass away, not the smallest letter or stroke shall pass from the Law until all is accomplished.

Fulfill in this verse does not mean to end. *Definition of* **fulfill**

to make full : to put into effect : to meet the requirements of : to convert into reality : to develop the full potentialities Synonyms = answer, complete, comply (with), fill, keep, meet, redeem, satisfy

Matthew 3:14-15–[14] But John tried to prevent Him, saying, "I have need to be baptized by You, and do You come to me?" [15] But Jesus answering said to him, "Permit *it* at this time; for in this way it is fitting for us to fulfill all righteousness." Then he *permitted Him.

So, did Jesus do away with any of the 10 commandments? The answer is a definite NO! **John 14:15–**"If you love Me, you will keep My commandments.

If you follow the ten commandments, it will not get you to Jesus. But, focus on Jesus and you will automatically follow the 10 commandments. So, don't just follow the 10 commandments, focus and follow Jesus.

Here are the 10 commandments

1–No other gods before Me. In view of His sovereignty and goodness (vs. 2), we are commanded to have no other gods before the Lord.

Exodus 20:3–"You shall have no other gods before Me."

2–You shall not make for yourself a carved image. The first and second commandments go hand in hand, both emphasizing the need to give our worship exclusively to the one true God. The Israelites violated this commandment and crafted their own graven image, a golden calf, even before Moses came down from the Mountain.

Exodus 20:4-6–"You shall not make for yourself an idol, or any likeness of what is in heaven above or on the earth beneath or in the water under the earth.. 5 You shall not worship them or serve them; for I, the LORD your God, am a jealous God, visiting the iniquity of the fathers on the children, on the third and the fourth generations of those who hate Me, 6 but showing lovingkindness to thousands, to those who love Me and keep My commandments."

3–You shall not take the name of the Lord your God in vain. To take God's name in vain is to use it in an empty or meaningless way. Because "there is no other name under heaven given among men by which we must be saved," we must be careful to instead treat the name of God with honor and reverence **Acts 4:12**–And there is salvation in no one else; for there is no other name under heaven that has been given among men by which we must be saved."

Exodus 20:7–"You shall not take the name of the LORD your God in vain, for the LORD will not leave him unpunished who takes His name in vain.."

4–Remember the Sabbath day.

Exodus 20:8-11–"Remember the Sabbath day, to keep it holy. [9] Six days you shall labor and do all your work, [10] but the seventh day is a Sabbath of the LORD your God; *in it* you shall not do any work, you or your son or your daughter, your male or your female servant or your cattle or your sojourner who stays with you. [11] For in six days the LORD made the heavens and the earth, the sea and all that is in them, and rested on the seventh day; therefore the LORD blessed the Sabbath day and made it holy.."

In wisdom and grace, God commanded His people to observe the seventh day as a day of rest. The Sabbath was to be observed in honor of God's own work in Creation (Exodus 20:11), as well as His redemptive work **Deuteronomy 5:15**–You shall remember that you were a slave in the land of Egypt, and the LORD your God brought you out of there by a mighty hand and by an outstretched arm; therefore the LORD your God commanded you to observe the Sabbath day.

5–Honor your father and your mother.

Exodus 20:12–"Honor your father and your mother, that your days may be prolonged in the land which the LORD your God gives you.."

The fifth commandment is reiterated by the apostle Paul who describes it as "the first commandment with promise" **Ephesians 6:2**– HONOR YOUR FATHER AND MOTHER (which is the first commandment with a promise), Honoring God means honoring the authority He has placed in our lives.

6–You shall not murder.

Exodus 20:13–"You shall not murder."

The taking of human life is expressly forbidden. Jesus elaborates on this commandment in the Sermon on the Mount, revealing that the sin of murder begins in the heart **Matthew 5:21-22–**[21] "You have heard that the ancients were told, 'YOU SHALL NOT COMMIT MURDER' and 'Whoever commits murder shall be liable to the court.' [22] But I say to you that everyone who is angry with his brother shall be guilty before the court; and whoever says to his brother, 'You good-for-nothing,' shall be guilty before the supreme court; and whoever says, 'You fool,' shall be guilty *enough to go* into the fiery hell.

7–You shall not commit adultery.

Exodus 20:14–"You shall not commit adultery."

The sanctity of marriage is given noteworthy attention throughout Scripture. Christ reminds us in Matthew 5:27-30 that the marriage relationship must be guarded diligently. **Matthew 5:27-30** [27] "You have heard that it was said, 'YOU SHALL NOT COMMIT ADULTERY'; [28] but I say to you that everyone who looks at a woman with lust for her has already committed adultery with her in his heart. [29] If your right eye makes you stumble, tear it out and throw it from you; for it is better for you to lose one of the parts of your body, than for your whole body to be thrown into hell. [30] If your right hand makes you stumble, cut it off and throw it from you; for it is better for you to lose one of the parts of your body, than for your whole body to go into hell.

8–You shall not steal.

Exodus 20:15–"You shall not steal."

Theft is forbidden by God. Instead, we are to be content with what we have and trust God to supply all our need in Christ Jesus **1 Timothy 6:6**–⁶ But godliness *actually* is a means of great gain when accompanied by contentment. **Philippians 4:19**–And my God will supply all your needs according to His riches in glory in Christ Jesus.

9–You shall not bear false witness.

Exodus 20:16–"You shall not bear false witness against your neighbor."

Honesty must always characterize our speech and conduct. To bear false witness against our neighbor is an affront to a holy God Who is Himself "the truth and the life" **John 14:6** Jesus *said to him, "I am the way, and the truth, and the life; no one comes to the Father but through Me.

10–You shall not covet.

Exodus 20:17–"You shall not covet your neighbor's house; you shall not covet your neighbor's wife or his male servant or his female servant or his ox or his donkey or anything that belongs to your neighbor."

God has promised to meet all our needs, both spiritual and physical, and we should therefore be content with whatever He has provided **Philippians 4:19**–And my God will supply all your needs according to His riches in glory in Christ Jesus.; **Matthew**

6:33–But seek first His kingdom and His righteousness, and all these things will be added to you. **Hebrews 13:5**–*Make sure that your character is free from the love of money, being content with what you have; for He Himself has said, "I* WILL NEVER DESERT YOU, NOR WILL I EVER FORSAKE YOU,*"*

Ecclesiastes 12:13–The conclusion, when all has been heard, *is*: fear God and keep His commandments, because this *applies to every person.*

Ephesians 2:8–For by grace you have been saved through faith; and that not of yourselves, *it is* the gift of God;

One of the arguments against the 10 commandments is that we are not under the law, we are under grace. Romans 3:28-31–²⁸ For we maintain that a man is justified by faith apart from works of the Law. ²⁹ Or is God *the God* of Jews only? Is He not *the God* of Gentiles also? Yes, of Gentiles also, ³⁰ since indeed God who will justify the circumcised by faith and the uncircumcised through faith is one. ³¹ Do we then nullify the Law through faith? May it never be! On the contrary, we establish the Law. **Romans 6:14-15** ¹⁴ For sin shall not be master over you, for you are not under law but under grace. ¹⁵ What then? Shall we sin because we are not under law but under grace? May it never be!

Grace is the power of God. We are not saved by the law, but we are saved by grace. We will not get to heaven by following the law, but, when we focus on Jesus, we will automatically follow the rules. So, don't just follow the rules, focus on and follow Jesus.

Daniel prophecies that the anti-christ (Daniel's little horn) will change LAWS and TIMES **Daniel 7:25** He will speak out against the Most High and wear down the saints of the Highest One, and he will intend to make alterations in times and in law; and they will be given into his hand for a time, times, and half a time. According to Daniel's prophecy, the anti-christ will change laws and times. But these 10 commandments will stay the same, no ore and no less, and Saturday is still the Sabbath of the 4th commandment. God does not change. **Malachi 3:6** "For I, the LORD, do not change; therefore you, O sons of Jacob, are not consumed. **Hebrews 13:8** Jesus Christ *is* the same yesterday and today and forever. **Matthew 5:18** For truly I say to you, until heaven and earth pass away, not the smallest letter

or stroke shall pass from the Law until all is accomplished.

Another argument that people use against the 10 commandments is they say that the law has been nailed to the cross. They are confused as to what laws have been nailed to the cross. There are two types of laws. There is God's law, which is the 10 commandments and was written on stone by God's finger and there is Moses' law, which are the ordinances. The ordinances were written by Moses on scrolls. The ordinances included the extra sabbaths and all of the sacrifices that were associated. The ordinances (laws) were what were nailed to the cross. **Colossians 2:14-15** [14] having canceled out the certificate of debt consisting of decrees against us, which was hostile to us; and He has taken it out of the way, having nailed it to the cross. [15] When He had disarmed the rulers and authorities, He made a public display of them, having triumphed over them through Him.

Deuteronomy 31:9–So Moses wrote this law and gave it to the priests, the sons of Levi who carried the ark of the covenant of the LORD, and to all the elders of Israel. **Deuteronomy 31:24-26**–[24] It came about, when Moses finished writing the words of this law in a book until they were complete, [25] that Moses commanded the

Levites who carried the ark of the covenant of the LORD, saying, [26] "Take this book of the law and place it **beside the ark of the covenant** of the LORD your God, that it may remain there as a witness against you.

Moses' laws (ordinances) were placed beside the Ark of the covenant.

Deuteronomy 10:1-5–The Tablets Rewritten "At that time the LORD said to me, 'Cut out for yourself two tablets of stone like the former ones, and come up to Me on the mountain, and make an ark of wood for yourself. [2]**I will write on the tablets the words that were on the former tablets which you shattered, and you shall put them in the ark**.' [3] So I made an ark of acacia wood and cut out two tablets of stone like the former ones, and went up on the mountain with the two tablets in my hand. [4] He wrote on the tablets, like the former writing, the Ten Commandments which the LORD had spoken to you on the mountain from the midst of the fire on the day of the assembly; and the LORD gave them to me. [5] Then I turned and came down from the mountain and put the tablets in the ark which I had made; and there they are, as the LORD commanded me."

So the Laws that God wrote were put inside the Ark of the covenant, while the ordinances that Moses wrote were put beside the Ark.

Moses's ordinances were fulfilled with Jesus.

1 John 5:2-3 [2] By this we know that we love the children of God, when we love God and observe His commandments. [3] For this is the love of God, that we keep His commandments; and His commandments are not burdensome.

The 10 commandments are very important. The first four are about God and the last 6 are about man. Jesus re-states this in the gospels

Matt 22:37-39. And He said to him, "'YOU SHALL LOVE THE LORD YOUR GOD WITH ALL YOUR HEART, AND WITH ALL YOUR SOUL, AND WITH ALL YOUR MIND.' ³⁸ This is the great and foremost commandment. ³⁹ The second is like it, 'YOU SHALL LOVE YOUR NEIGHBOR AS YOURSELF.' Jesus did not change the commandments. He just summed them up in two verses.

The 4th commandment is the longest (in Exodus) and is about the 7th day (Sabbath). The Sabbath is the first thing the God made Holy **Genesis 2:3** Then God blessed the seventh day and sanctified it, because in it He rested from all His work which God had created and made.

Isaiah 58:13-14 Keeping the Sabbath

"If because of the Sabbath, you turn your foot From doing your *own* pleasure on My holy day,

And call the Sabbath a delight, the holy *day* of the LORD honorable, And honor it, desisting from your *own* ways, From seeking your *own* pleasure And speaking *your own* word, Then you will take delight in the LORD, And I will make you ride on the heights of the earth; And I will feed you *with* the heritage of Jacob your father, For the mouth of the LORD has spoken."

So, Yes, the 10 commandments are very important. They have been an important building block for America and we should not forget them.

Chapter 11

ARE THERE RULES FOR PRAYER?

∞

A ccording to Matthew 6:6 we are to pray in secret and not in the open for other people to hear. We are not to use "vain repetitions" and when we pray, we are to pray prayers similar to the Lord's prayer. Jesus taught the disciples the Lords prayer, when the disciples asked him to teach them to pray.

Matthew 6:9-15

[9] "Pray, then, in this way:
'Our Father who is in heaven, Hallowed be Your name.
[10] 'Your kingdom come. Your will be done, On earth as it is in heaven.
[11] 'Give us this day our daily bread.
[12] 'And forgive us our debts, as we also have forgiven our debtors.
[13] 'And do not lead us into temptation, but deliver us from evil. [For Yours is the kingdom and the power and the glory forever. Amen.']

[14] For if you forgive others for their transgressions, your heavenly Father will also forgive you. [15] But if you do not forgive others, then your Father will not forgive your transgressions.

The Lord's Prayer was given as a model for prayer. Jesus was teaching against the vain repetitious prayers of hypocrites. The prayer has words of praise, confession, thanks giving, and supplication.

We offer our prayers to the Father to thank Him for all that He has done for us, to partition Him for things we are in need of and close our prayer in the name of Jesus Christ. Many people recite the Lords Prayer, but they forget that Christ only gave them this as a guide as to what to say, and not to use it as an actual prayer.

What you ask for or thank Him for in your prayer does not have to be the same each time. You pray as guided by the Spirit.

Jesus' prayer can be read in the Gospel of John, chapter 17. Most confuse the 'Lord's Prayer' found here with what is properly called the 'model' prayer found in Matthew 5 given by Jesus as a way for us to pray to our 'Father.'

John 17:1-5 The High Priestly Prayer

Jesus spoke these things; and lifting up His eyes to heaven, He said, "Father, the hour has come; glorify Your Son, that the Son may glorify You, [2] even as You gave Him authority over all flesh, that to all whom You have given Him, He may give eternal life. [3] This is eternal life, that they may know You, the only true God, and Jesus Christ whom You have sent. [4] I glorified You on the earth, having accomplished the work which You have given Me to do. [5] Now, Father, glorify Me together with Yourself, with the glory which I had with You before the world was.

Matthew 5:1-11 The Sermon on the Mount; The Beatitudes

5 When Jesus saw the crowds, He went up on the mountain; and after He sat down, His disciples came to Him. ² He opened His mouth and *began* to teach them, saying,

³ "ᶦBlessed are the poor in spirit, for theirs is the kingdom of heaven.

⁴ "Blessed are those who mourn, for they shall be comforted.

⁵ "Blessed are the gentle, for they shall inherit the earth.

⁶ "Blessed are those who hunger and thirst for righteousness, for they shall be satisfied.

⁷ "Blessed are the merciful, for they shall receive mercy.

⁸ "Blessed are the pure in heart, for they shall see God.

⁹ "Blessed are the peacemakers, for they shall be called sons of God.

¹⁰ "Blessed are those who have been persecuted for the sake of righteousness, for theirs is the kingdom of heaven.

¹¹ "Blessed are you when *people* insult you and persecute you, and falsely say all kinds of evil against you because of Me. ¹² Rejoice and be glad, for your reward in heaven is great; for in the same way they persecuted the prophets who were before you.

[God's Prayer Rules are Simple but Not Easy]

"I got nothing that I asked for, but everything that I could have ever hoped for." Most people do not believe that they got everything in life that they could have ever hoped for. God has one of three answers for all prayers: "Your way, My way, or No way."

All People, Christians and heathens alike believe that they can change the mind of a Sovereign God Who always knows long in advance how He will fulfill His perfect plan and purpose under every and all circumstances. Many imagine that answered prayer is when God changes His mind with regards to the way things were going in your life. In other words: You change your ways to please God, and God will change His mind and begin blessing you. NOT TRUE. God never, ever changes His mind about anything.

Malachi 3:6 "For I, the LORD, do not change;

If you like drama, then Matt. 26:36 is the place to find it.

Matthew 26:36 The Garden of Gethsemane Then Jesus came with them to a place called Gethsemane, and *said to His disciples, "Sit here while I go over there and pray."

After praying for one hour Jesus returns a short way back to His Apostles and says:

Matthew 26:41 Keep watching and praying that you may not enter into temptation; the spirit is willing, but the flesh is weak."

Was the "flesh" of Jesus any stronger than that of His apostles? No, it was the same flesh.

1 Corinthians 15:39 All flesh is not the same flesh, but there is one *flesh* of men, and another flesh of beasts, and another flesh of birds, and another of fish.

Jesus was given this same **"one kind"** of flesh

John 1:14 The Word Made Flesh

[14] And the Word became flesh, and dwelt among us, and we saw His glory, glory as of the only begotten from the Father, full of grace and truth.

Romans 1:3 concerning His Son, who was born of a descendant of David according to the flesh,

And so the flesh of Jesus was just as **"weak"** as that of His Apostles. Jesus instructed His apostles to stay awake and pray with Him for one hour.

Mark 14:32-42 Jesus in Gethsemane

[32] They *came to a place named Gethsemane; and He *said to His disciples, "Sit here until I have prayed." [33] And He *took with Him Peter and James and John, and began to be very distressed and troubled. [34] And He *said to them, "My soul is deeply grieved to the point of death; remain here and keep watch." [35] And He went a little beyond *them*, and fell to the ground and *began* to pray that if it were possible, the hour might pass Him by. [36] And He was saying, **"Abba! Father! All things are possible for You; remove this cup from Me; yet not what I will, but what You will."** [37] And He *came and *found them sleeping, and *said to Peter, "Simon, are you asleep? Could you not keep watch for one hour? [38] Keep watching and praying that you may not come into temptation; the spirit is willing, but the flesh is weak." [39] Again He went away and prayed, saying the same words. [40] And again He came and found them sleeping, for their eyes were very heavy; and they did not know what to answer Him. [41] And He *came the third time, and *said to them, "Are you still sleeping and resting? It is enough; the hour has come; behold, the Son of Man is being betrayed into the hands of sinners. [42] Get up, let us be going; behold, the one who betrays Me is at hand!"

Luke 22:43-44 [43] Now an angel from heaven appeared to Him, strengthening Him. [44] And being in agony He was praying very fervently; and His sweat became like drops of blood, falling down upon the ground.

I doubt that any of us can ever fully appreciate what unfathomable human trauma and agony was taking place for those three hours in the garden that night two thousand years ago. The eternal destiny of the entire human race was at stake, and Jesus KNEW IT! And God was agonizing with him.

Isaiah 63:9 In all their affliction He was afflicted, And the angel of His presence saved them;

In His love and in His mercy He redeemed them, And He lifted them and carried them all the days of old.

Hebrews 5:8 Although He was a Son, He learned obedience from the things which He suffered.

Christ was suffering that night in the garden! But there in the garden is the answer to all prayer. "Abba! Father! All things are possible for You; remove this cup from Me; **yet not what I will, but what You will.**" Jesus not only prayed that way; Jesus thought that way:

John 5:30 "I can do nothing on My own initiative. As I hear, I judge; and My judgment is just, because I do not seek My own will, but the will of Him who sent Me.

And to repeat:

John 6:38 For I have come down from heaven, not to do My own will, but the will of Him who sent Me.

Jesus prayed as earnestly as it is possible to pray that God would **"let this cup pass?"**

Did God grant Jesus His desire to **"let this cup pass?"** NO, He did not.

But, did Jesus get His prayer answered? YES, He surely did. because Jesus' greater desire was that His Father's will be done, rather than **"let this cup pass."** This example from our Lord is the answer to answered prayer and it is also the answer to unanswered prayer.

If you always pray, **"not as I will, but as THOU will,"** all of your prayers will be answered too. Whether you always get what you desire or you don't get what you desire, if your greatest desire of all desires is for **"THY WILL be done,"** then you can rest assured that from this day forward, all of your prayers will be answered always. God's will–will always be done. No prayer has ever changed God's plan or purpose in any way whatsoever.

God's will must be done, and if that is the greatest desire of your prayer for God's will to be done in your life, THEN YOUR PRAYER WILL BE ANSWERED.

God has never made a mistake. God has never ever changed His mind. When God wants to answer someone's prayer, the first thing He will always do is inspire that person TO PRAY.

SEVEN PRINCIPLES ABOUT PRAYER
FROM SCRIPTURE

[1] We need to do everything according to his purpose and plan or it won't happen

Ephesians 1:11 also we have obtained an inheritance, having been predestined according to His purpose who works all things after the counsel of His will,

1 John 5:14-15 [14] This is the confidence which we have before Him, that, if we ask anything according to His will, He hears us. [15] And if we know that He hears us *in* whatever we ask, we know that we have the requests which we have asked from Him.

[2] If our heart condemns us not

1 John 3:21-22 [21] Beloved, if our heart does not condemn us, we have confidence before God; [22] and whatever we ask we receive from Him, because we keep His commandments and do the things that are pleasing in His sight.

[3] keep His commandments, and do those things that are pleasing in His sight...

Revelation 14:12 Here is the perseverance of the saints who keep the commandments of God and their faith in Jesus.

[4] And this is His commandment, That we should believe on the Name of His Son Jesus Christ...

1 John 3:23 This is His commandment, that we believe in the name of His Son Jesus Christ, and love one another, just as He commanded us.

[5] And <u>love one another</u>, as He gave us commandment"

John 13:34-35 [34] A new commandment I give to you, that you love one another, even as I have loved you, that you also love one another. [35] By this all men will know that you are My disciples, if you have love for one another."

Deuteronomy 6:5 You shall love the LORD your God with all your heart and with all your soul and with all your might.

[6] "Ye ask, and receive not, because ye ask amiss, that ye may <u>consume it upon your lusts</u> [so don't think that it's okay to pray for your Mother to hit the Lotto Jackpot either, as I believe that God can see through such feigned benevolence] ".

James 4:3 You ask and do not receive, because you ask with wrong motives, so that you may spend *it* on your pleasures.

[7] Have faith and trust, not just hoping and wishing. True faith can be based only on God's Word

James 1:6-7 [6] But he must ask in faith without any doubting, for the one who doubts is like the surf of the sea, driven and tossed by the wind. [7] For that man ought not to expect that he will receive anything from the Lord,

All seven of these principles are in keeping with **"Thy will be done."**

HERE ARE MORE SCRIPTURES
CONCERNING PRAYER

Romans 8:24-26

²⁴ For in hope we have been saved, but hope that is seen is not hope; for who hopes for what he *already* sees? ²⁵ But if we hope for what we do not see, with perseverance we wait eagerly for it.

Our Victory in Christ

²⁶ In the same way the Spirit also helps our weakness; for we do not know how to pray as we should, but the Spirit Himself intercedes for *us* with groanings too deep for words;

Romans 8:27-28 ²⁷ and He who searches the hearts knows what the mind of the Spirit is, because He intercedes for the saints according to *the will of* God.

²⁸ And we know that God causes all things to work together for good to those who love God, to those who are called according to *His* purpose.

James 1:17 Every good thing given and every perfect gift is from above, coming down from the Father of lights, with whom there is no variation or shifting shadow.

We know not what we should pray for, but it must be in God's will.

Matthew 6:10 'Your kingdom come. Your will be done, On earth as it is in heaven.

John 6:51 I am the living bread that came down out of heaven; if anyone eats of this bread, he will live forever; and the bread also which I will give for the life of the world is My flesh."

SO WHAT SHOULD WE PRAY FOR?

Pray for anything that is in God's will. Qualities of godliness, love, faith, courage, knowledge and understanding, wisdom, patience, self-control, thankfulness, and the well-being and health of others. Pray about anything and everything that falls within God's will and weighs on you mind

Speak to God as often as possible and anywhere.

Build a close relationship with he Holy Spirit and speak to God often. Anything important enough for you to be concerned about is worthy of talking with God about.

Be sure to thank God for everything. EVERYTHING!

Pray for safety of friends, family and also the people who protect us like the police and military.

1 Timothy 6:8 If we have food and covering, with these we shall be content.

Philippians 4:4-9

[4] Rejoice in the Lord always; again I will say, rejoice! [5] Let your gentle *spirit* be known to all men. The Lord is near. [6] Be anxious for nothing, but in everything by prayer and supplication with thanksgiving let your requests be made known to God. [7] And the peace of

God, which surpasses all comprehension, will guard your hearts and your minds in Christ Jesus.

[8] Finally, brethren, whatever is true, whatever is honorable, whatever is right, whatever is pure, whatever is lovely, whatever is of good repute, if there is any excellence and if anything worthy of praise, dwell on these things. [9] The things you have learned and received and heard and seen in me, practice these things, and the God of peace will be with you.

1 Thessalonians 5:17 pray without ceasing;

In his famous book *Institutes of the Christian Religion*, Calvin outlines what he calls the five rules for "right" prayer.

John Calvin on Prayer: 5 Rules

Rule #1: Pray with reverence.

You should recognize (quickly) who God is, and who we are. "Now for framing prayer duly and properly, let this be the first rule: that we be disposed in mind and heart as befits those who enter conversation with God," writes Calvin. Yes, our supplications matter. But we start with reverence.

Calvin adds: "Let us therefore realize that the only persons who duly and properly gird themselves to pray are those who are so moved by God's majesty that, freed from earthly cares and affections, they come to it." When you understand God's bigness and your smallness, you'll come to prayer with the right posture — namely, with reverence.

Rule# 2: Pray from a sincere sense of want, and with recognition of your insufficiency.

Prayer is a reminder that we are insufficient, and we are dependent on the all-sufficiency of Christ. Calvin uses the word "penitent" to describe the right attitude. To be "penitent" means to feel or express sorrow for sin. But Calvin also adds it's okay to ask for things, if we ask with a sincere sense of want, and a right understanding of God.

"Let each one, therefore, as he prepares to pray, be displeased with his own evil deeds (something that cannot happen without repentance), and let him take the person and disposition of a beggar."

Rule #3: Pray without confidence in yourself and humbly plead for pardon.

One sentence says it all. "Anyone who stands before God to pray, in his humility giving glory completely to God, should abandon all thoughts of his own glory, cast off all notion of his own worth, in fine, put away all self-assurance — lest if we claim for ourselves anything, even the least bit, we should become mainly puffed up, and perish at his presence."

Rule #4: Pray with confident hope in God.

"Thus cast down and overcome by true humility, we should be nonetheless encouraged to pray by a sure hope that our prayer will be answered," says Calvin.

Don't let the first three rules discourage you. One of the bright spot's of Calvin's theology is his right understanding of the majesty of God. Yet, in this third step, Calvin is beginning to soften a little, and begin to allow us to pray according to our childlike stance with God.

He continues: "And although Satan tries to block all paths to prevent them from prayer, they should nonetheless break through, surely persuaded that, although not freed from all hindrances, their efforts still please God and their petitions are approved."

Rule #5: Pray in Jesus' name.

We pray in Jesus' name not be to cliché, but because we recognize that Jesus is our advocate before the Father. "For as soon as God's dread majesty comes to mind, we cannot but tremble and be driven far away by the recognition of our own unworthiness, until Christ comes forward as the intermediary, to change the throne of dreadful glory into the throne of grace."

Seven Laws of Prayer

God Does Not Hear Us at Random

In nature, everything works according to set laws. It is the same in the spiritual realm: God acts according to laws. So often we get discouraged and believe that prayer is useless when our prayers do not get answered. However, the actual reason is that we have not fulfilled God's laws which are a condition for prayer.

1. The Law of a Pure Heart

Hebrews 10:22 let us draw near with a sincere heart in full assurance of faith, having our hearts sprinkled *clean* from an evil conscience and our bodies washed with pure water.

God's first condition is that my heart must be pure. **Psalm 66:18** If I regard wickedness in my heart, The Lord will not hear;

Isaiah 1:15 "So when you spread out your hands *in prayer*, I will hide My eyes from you;

Yes, even though you multiply prayers, I will not listen. Your hands are covered with blood.

Sin in your heart will close God's ear and cut off all communication with Him. It is useless for me to pray when I am carrying a sin on my conscience which I have not yet acknowledged. I might as well get up from my knees if there is anything in my life which I know is contrary to the will of God.

Joshua 7:10-12 [10] So the LORD said to Joshua, "Rise up! Why is it that you have fallen on your face? [11] Israel has sinned, and they have also transgressed My covenant which I commanded them. And they have even taken some of the things under the ban and have both stolen and deceived. Moreover, they have also put *them* among their own things. [12] Therefore the sons of Israel cannot stand before their enemies; they turn *their* backs before their enemies, for they have become accursed. I will not be with you anymore unless you destroy the things under the ban from your midst.

The Lord told Joshua to stop praying. Why? Because He does not want to communicate with a soul that remains in sin. Repentance and cleansing from sin are essential for fellowship with God.

2. The Law of a Forgiving Spirit

This is a condition for getting your prayers answered. **Mark 11:25** Whenever you stand praying, forgive, if you have anything against anyone, so that your Father who is in heaven will also forgive you your transgressions.

I fear that the spirit of unforgiveness is more widespread than one would generally notice. Often you can find it with people who are, outwardly, very sincere, and who take an active part in the work of the Lord; even these people can harbor a spirit of unforgiveness towards somebody else. If we are not prepared to forgive, our prayer will not be acceptable to God. A forgiving spirit is so essential that the Lord made a drastic statement in Mark: "But if ye do not forgive, neither will your Father which is in heaven forgive you your trespasses" **Mark 11:26** [But if you do not forgive, neither will your Father who is in heaven forgive your transgressions."] **Matthew 6:15** But if you do not forgive others, then your Father will not forgive your transgressions.

I will not try to explain this mysterious statement of the Lord. However, in the light of it, I search my own heart and watch and pray earnestly that I will never be guilty of this horrible sin, and that I will never be subject to this terrible judgment.

3. The Law of the Right Motive

James 4:3 You ask and do not receive, because you ask with wrong motives, so that you may spend *it* on your pleasures.

I can go to God and ask Him for things which are completely in order: e.g. I can ask Him to use the Gospel for the salvation of souls, to let evangelization prosper, but if my motive is my own pleasure, my own wealth or the approval of people, my prayer will not be answered.

Can I rejoice as much as though God had used myself? If I cannot do this, my motive for praying is wrong.

If my prayer is to be victorious prayer, which guarantees an answer, it is not to be inspired by the desire for selfish pleasure or success.

A proper motive is essential in order to receive an answer to our prayer. And there is only one reason to pray which is right–namely: "That God in all things may be glorified" **1 Peter 4:11** Whoever speaks, *is to do so* as one who is speaking the utterances of God; whoever serves *is to do so* as one who is serving by the strength which God supplies; so that in all things God may be glorified through Jesus Christ, to whom belongs the glory and dominion forever and ever. Amen.

1 Corinthians 10:31 Whether, then, you eat or drink or whatever you do, do all to the glory of God.

4. The Law of Faith

"Let him ask in faith, nothing wavering..." **James 1:6** But he must ask in faith without any doubting, for the one who doubts is like the surf of the sea, driven and tossed by the wind. Weymouth translates this as: "Let him... have no doubts." Faith is indispensable if we want to receive answers to our prayers, for "without faith it is impossible to please him" **Hebrews 11:6** And without faith it is impossible to please *Him*, for he who comes to God must believe that He is and *that* He is a rewarder of those who seek Him.

However, when there is faith, God works miracles.

In the Gospel of Mark our Lord gave an amazing promise to the praying soul: **Mark 11:23** Truly I say to you, whoever says to this mountain, 'Be taken up and cast into the sea,' and does not doubt in his heart, but believes that what he says is going to happen, it will be *granted* him.

How many of us have prayed that the mountains which block the spreading of the Gospel should be removed! Yet, how few of us have seen these mountains being cast into the sea? Why? Because of our unbelief.

5. Pray According to the Will of God

"If we ask any thing according to his will, he hears us" **1 John 5:14** This is the confidence which we have before Him, that, if we ask anything according to His will, He hears us.

Everything depends on this. First we have to find out God's will, and we have to pray according to His will. Without knowing God's will it is impossible to have faith that moves mountains.

Paul's prayer for the Colossians was that they "might be filled with the knowledge of his will" **Colossians 1:9** For this reason also, since the day we heard *of it*, we have not ceased to pray for you and to ask that you may be filled with the knowledge of His will in all spiritual wisdom and understanding,

This requires an intimate knowledge of God Himself. How do we get to know the desires of our friends? By talking to them, and by being with them often. How do we get to know God's will? By five-minute-prayers? No! It is by waiting, waiting, and waiting on God. We cannot get to know the will of God within five minutes, perhaps not even in five hours, and possibly not even in five days.

It is a matter of waiting before God daily, and learning His will for that day. It is constantly visiting with the Holy Spirit.

6. Praying in the Name of Jesus

Jesus said: **John 14:14** If you ask Me anything in My name, I will do *it*.

What a promise!

But what does it mean, to ask in the Name of Jesus? Something much deeper than some people think. It is not a matter of quoting a formula.

To ask in the Name of Jesus means to ask for things Jesus would like. God will never say no to this: He cannot, because He loves His Son; and when we pray in the Name of Jesus our prayer must be answered, even if it means moving a mountain.

7. Praying in the Holy Spirit

"Praying in the Holy Spirit" **Jude 20** But you, beloved, building yourselves up on your most holy faith, praying in the Holy Spirit,

This is the secret of every victorious prayer. It is impossible to ask in faith if we are not controlled and inspired by the Holy Spirit. The Holy Spirit is the only one who can give faith; He is the only one who knows what Jesus wants, the only one who can reveal the will of God.

How can we pray in the Holy Spirit? The secret can be found in **Galatians 5:25** If we live by the Spirit, let us also walk by the Spirit.

: "If we live in the Spirit, let us also walk in the Spirit." Before we can pray in the Holy Spirit, we must learn to walk in the Spirit; to live in unbroken fellowship with God, every day and every hour of the day, in fact "moment by moment".

Only then, once we have learnt to do that, will we always be able to pray with a pure heart, with a forgiving spirit, with the right motive, with unreserved faith, according to the will of God, and in the Name of Jesus. Then, and only then, can we receive answers to our prayers. Then "it shall happen". Then we will be able to challenge every mountain in the Name of the Lord Jesus.

Provided that we walk in the Spirit, nothing, NOTHING, **NOTHING** will be impossible to us.

Lord, teach us to pray!

1 Thessalonians 5:17 pray without ceasing;

Chapter 12

CLIMATE CHANGE IS NOT NEW

∞

One of the big topics from the left is climate change. It started
out a couple of decades ago as "global warming". When that
failed and the glaciers and ice caps started to grow they changed the
name to "climate change". Liberal politicians are presenting "climate change" as something that man can control. The first example
of "climate change" in history is "the flood".

Genesis 7:1-5, 17-24 The Flood

Then the LORD said to Noah, "Enter the ark, you and all your household, for you *alone* I have seen *to be* righteous before Me in this
time. ² You shall take with you of every clean animal by sevens, a
male and his female; and of the animals that are not clean two, a
male and his female; ³ also of the birds of the sky, by sevens, male
and female, to keep offspring alive on the face of all the earth. ⁴
For after seven more days, I will send rain on the earth forty days
and forty nights; and I will blot out from the face of the land every
living thing that I have made." ⁵ Noah did according to all that the
LORD had commanded him.

[17] Then the flood came upon the earth for forty days, and the water increased and lifted up the ark, so that it rose above the earth. [18] The water prevailed and increased greatly upon the earth, and the ark floated on the surface of the water. [19] The water prevailed more and more upon the earth, so that all the high mountains everywhere under the heavens were covered. [20] The water prevailed fifteen cubits higher, and the mountains were covered. [21] All flesh that moved on the earth perished, birds and cattle and beasts and every swarming thing that swarms upon the earth, and all mankind; [22] of all that was on the dry land, all in whose nostrils was the breath of the spirit of life, died. [23] Thus He blotted out every living thing that was upon the face of the land, from man to animals to creeping things and to birds of the sky, and they were blotted out from the earth; and only Noah was left, together with those that were with him in the ark. [24] The water prevailed upon the earth one hundred and fifty days.

Liberal politicians are presenting global warming, global cooling, climate change as being man-made. climate change has been happening for thousands of years. It is all up to God, not man. "Climate change" is not created by man. More proof–3 thousand years ago God told Joseph about the drought that was going to happen. Joseph told the Pharoah and they stored 7 years worth of grain. The drought happened and storing the grain saved the people. Genesis 41:46-57

Genesis 41:46-49, 53-57

[46] Now Joseph was thirty years old when he stood before Pharaoh, king of Egypt. And Joseph went out from the presence of Pharaoh and went through all the land of Egypt. [47] During the seven years of plenty the land brought forth abundantly. [48] So he gathered all the food of *these* seven years which occurred in the land of Egypt and

placed the food in the cities; he placed in every city the food from its own surrounding fields. [49] Thus Joseph stored up grain in great abundance like the sand of the sea, until he stopped measuring *it*, for it was beyond measure.

[53] When the seven years of plenty which had been in the land of Egypt came to an end, [54] and the seven years of famine began to come, just as Joseph had said, then there was famine in all the lands, but in all the land of Egypt there was bread. [55] So when all the land of Egypt was famished, the people cried out to Pharaoh for bread; and Pharaoh said to all the Egyptians, "Go to Joseph; whatever he says to you, you shall do." [56] When the famine was *spread* over all the face of the earth, then Joseph opened all the storehouses, and sold to the Egyptians; and the famine was severe in the land of Egypt. [57] *The people of* all the earth came to Egypt to buy grain from Joseph, because the famine was severe in all the earth.

1 Kings 17:1-9 Elijah Predicts Drought

17 [1] Now Elijah the Tishbite, who was of the settlers of Gilead, said to Ahab, "As the Lord, the God of Israel lives, before whom I stand, surely there shall be neither dew nor rain these years, except by my word." [2] The word of the Lord came to him, saying, [3] "Go away from here and turn eastward, and hide yourself by the brook Cherith, which is east of the Jordan. [4] It shall be that you will drink of the brook, and I have commanded the ravens to provide for you there." [5] So he went and did according to the word of the Lord, for he went and lived by the brook Cherith, which is east of the Jordan. [6] The ravens brought him bread and meat in the morning and bread and meat in the evening, and he would drink from the brook. [7] It happened after a while that the brook dried up, because there was no rain in the land.

[8] Then the word of the L ORD came to him, saying, [9] "Arise, go to Zarephath, which belongs to Sidon, and stay there; behold, I have commanded a widow there to provide for you." [1]

The drought ended with Elijah against the prophets of baal.

1 Kings 18:20-40–God or Baal on Mount Carmel

[20] So Ahab sent *a message* among all the sons of Israel and brought the prophets together at Mount Carmel. [21] Elijah came near to all the people and said, "How long *will* you hesitate between two opinions? If the L ORD is God, follow Him; but if Baal, follow him." But the people did not answer him a word. [22] Then Elijah said to the people, "I alone am left a prophet of the L ORD, but Baal's prophets are 450 men. [23] Now let them give us two oxen; and let them choose one ox for themselves and cut it up, and place it on the wood, but put no fire *under it*; and I will prepare the other ox and lay it on the wood, and I will not put a fire *under it*. [24] Then you call on the name of your god, and I will call on the name of the L ORD, and the God who answers by fire, He is God." And all the people said, "That is a good idea."

[25] So Elijah said to the prophets of Baal, "Choose one ox for yourselves and prepare it first for you are many, and call on the name of your god, but put no fire *under it*." [26] Then they took the ox which was given them and they prepared it and called on the name of Baal from morning until noon saying, "O Baal, answer us." But there was no voice and no one answered. And they leaped about the altar which they made. [27] It came about at noon, that Elijah mocked them and said, "Call out with a loud voice, for he is a god; either he is occupied or gone aside, or is on a journey, or perhaps he is asleep and needs to be awakened." [28] So they cried with a loud voice and cut themselves according to their custom with swords and lances

until the blood gushed out on them. ²⁹ When midday was past, they raved until the time of the offering of the *evening* sacrifice; but there was no voice, no one answered, and no one paid attention.

³⁰ Then Elijah said to all the people, "Come near to me." So all the people came near to him. And he repaired the altar of the LORD which had been torn down. ³¹ Elijah took twelve stones according to the number of the tribes of the sons of Jacob, to whom the word of the LORD had come, saying, "Israel shall be your name." ³² So with the stones he built an altar in the name of the LORD, and he made a trench around the altar, large enough to hold two measures of seed. ³³ Then he arranged the wood and cut the ox in pieces and laid *it* on the wood. ³⁴ And he said, "Fill four pitchers with water and pour *it* on the burnt offering and on the wood." And he said, "Do it a second time," and they did it a second time. And he said, "Do it a third time," and they did it a third time. ³⁵ The water flowed around the altar and he also filled the trench with water.

Elijah's Prayer

³⁶ At the time of the offering of the *evening* sacrifice, Elijah the prophet came near and said, "O LORD, the God of Abraham, Isaac and Israel, today let it be known that You are God in Israel and that I am Your servant and I have done all these things at Your word. ³⁷ Answer me, O LORD, answer me, that this people may know that You, O LORD, are God, and *that* You have turned their heart back again." ³⁸ Then the fire of the LORD fell and consumed the burnt offering and the wood and the stones and the dust, and licked up the water that was in the trench. ³⁹ When all the people saw it, they fell on their faces; and they said, "The LORD, He is God; the LORD, He is God." ⁴⁰ Then Elijah said to them, "Seize the prophets of Baal; do not let one of them escape." So they seized them; and Elijah brought them down to the brook Kishon, and slew them there.

Man can not control the environment. Man can not control God. The most notable time that man tried to control God they built this tower in Babel (now Iraq) and everyone knows how that ended.

Genesis 11:4-9

[4]They said, "Come, let us build for ourselves a city, and a tower whose top *will reach* into heaven, and let us make for ourselves a name, otherwise we will be scattered abroad over the face of the whole earth." [5]The LORD came down to see the city and the tower which the sons of men had built. [6]The LORD said, "Behold, they are one people, and they all have the same language. And this is what they began to do, and now nothing which they purpose to do will be impossible for them. [7]Come, let Us go down and there confuse their language, so that they will not understand one another's speech." [8] So the LORD scattered them abroad from there over the face of the whole earth; and they stopped building the city. [9]Therefore its name was called Babel, because there the LORD confused the language of the whole earth; and from there the LORD scattered them abroad over the face of the whole earth.

Thinking that man can control the environment is just idiotic.

A little added note–the year that Al Gore was born there were 130,000 glaciers on earth. Today, there are only 130,000 glaciers on earth.

2014 was supposed to be the hottest year ever. If it actually was "hottest year ever" you'd think all the terrible calamities that are supposed to happen would be happening now but instead the opposite is happening.

Here are some facts from 2014

1. Record Ice

In 2014 there was record sea ice in Antarctica in fact a global warming expedition got stuck in it. Plus, the Arctic sea ice also made comeback in 2014. The Great lakes had record ice Lake Superior only had 3 ice free months in 2014.

2. Record Snow

2014 saw record snowfall in many areas, remember when they said that global warming would cause snow to disappear?.

3. Record Cold

In 2014 we saw all kinds of cold records remember the Polar Vortex? You'd think that we'd be breaking all kinds of heat records in "the hottest year ever"

4. Oceans Are Rising Much Less Than Predicted

5. Polar Bears Are Thriving

6. Moose Are Making A Comeback

A few years ago the moose population in Minnesota dropped rapidly and they immediately blamed global warming, then they did a study and found out it was actually wolves that were killing the moose. Wolves have been taken off the endangered species list and are now endangering other species so they opened a wolf hunting season in Minnesota and the moose are coming back. It turns out it had nothing to do with global warming in fact the years when the moose population declined were some very cold ones.

7. 99% of Scientists don't believe in Catastrophic Man-Made Global Warming

8. Nature produces much more CO2 than man

In 2014 NASA finally launched a satellite that measures CO2 levels around the globe. They assumed that most of the CO2 would be coming from the industrialized northern hemisphere but much to their surprise it was coming from the rainforests in South America, Africa and China.

Human-inspired "climate change" is a ruse. It is all a control-grabbing, land-grabbing, money-grabbing hoax. "Rising sea levels," "ocean change," and "global warming," (now referred to as "climate change") have become part of the vernacular despite severely flawed global warming models.

Chapter 13

PALESTINIANS ARE NOT LATTER-DAY PHILISTINES – THEY ARE JUST THORNS IN ISRAEL'S SIDE.

❧

The Palestinians were a nomadic people with no country.

Not only were they nomadic but they were hostile nomadic sent to Israel to fight the establishment of the pre-Jewish state and to fight in the wars. Palestinian and any other Arab nationality is a new invention. To the extremists within Islam there is only Ummat al Islam, Nation of Islam. They don't recognize sovereign nationalist borders.

The nations that the Palestinians actually come from are predominately Syria and minority from Egypt, but they also came from other Arab nations as well. Living in mud huts, those were favorable early on before modernization. Palestinian nationalism wasn't invented until the 60s when the Arabs lost their wars. The first full fledged war of nation v nation was in 1948 but they had waged many small wars previous to this.

The countries that waged war on fledgling Israel–May 14, 1948

Jordan–May 25, 1946, Syria–April 17, 1946, Lebanon–November 22, 1943, Egypt–February 18, 1922, Iraq–October 3, 1932, North Yemen 1918

The Palestinian people do not exist as a country. The creation of a Palestinian state is only a means for continuing the struggle against the state of Israel for Arab unity. In reality today there is no difference between Jordanians, Palestinians, Syrians and Lebanese.

Israeli and Palestinian Authority security sources are convinced that followers of ISIS in the Gaza Strip are responsible for some of the recent rocket attacks on Israel. Hamas seems to be losing control over the dozens of terror cells belonging to ISIS and other jihadi groups.

Meanwhile, what does Bible prophecy have to say about the Gaza Strip, which is a continual thorn in the side of Israel?

The region known as Gaza belonged to the ancient arch-enemies of Israel called the Philistines but was part of the territory apportioned to Judah. Gaza, or *Azza* in Hebrew, was a city on the southern coastal plain of *Eretz Yisrael* (the Land of Israel, today *Medinat Yisrael*, or the modern nation State of Israel.

In Biblical times, God gave this Holy Land as an eternal covenant that can never be broken to the Children of Israel (the descendants of Jacob). Highly contested by the Islamists, the deed of trust to Eretz Yisrael is documented in the Bible: Gaza was captured and conquered by the tribe of Judah: *"Also Judah took Gaza with the regions thereof, and Ashkelon with the regions thereof, and Ekron with the region thereof."* **Judges 1:18** And Judah took

Gaza with its territory and Ashkelon with its territory and Ekron with its territory.

, and it was included in the allotment to Judah's tribe **Joshua 15:47** Ashdod, its towns and its villages; Gaza, its towns and its villages; as far as the brook of Egypt and the Great Sea, even *its* coastline.

Here are a couple of other Scriptures that mention this troubled area on the coastline:

"The Philistines took [Samson], and put out his eyes, and brought him down to Gaza." **Judges 16:21** Then the Philistines seized him and gouged out his eyes; and they brought him down to Gaza and bound him with bronze chains, and he was a grinder in the prison. [Hezekiah of Judah] smote the Philistines even unto Gaza ... **2 Kings 18:8** He defeated the Philistines as far as Gaza and its territory, from watchtower to fortified city.

Today the ancient Philistines no longer exist; however the term rendered "Palestine" is literally, "the land of the Philistines," Isaiah 11:14 declares that Israel shall "fly upon the shoulders of the Philistines [i.e. Palestinians] toward the west [i.e. Gaza]..." **Isaiah 11:14** They will swoop down on the slopes of the Philistines on the west; Together they will plunder the sons of the east; They will possess Edom and Moab, And the sons of Ammon will be subject to them.

Israel continues to make incursions into Gaza, in retaliation for the many rockets that are fired daily from Gaza, and so it could be said that this prophecy of Isaiah 11:14 has more than one fulfillment.

Bible prophecy indicates there is an End-time Philistine power that God allows as an agent to goad Israel. The Isaiah 11 passage speaks of the Philistine power to "the west," which includes the territory currently occupied by the Palestinians.

Until Messiah returns, we can expect the Palestinians to continue their role as latter-day Philistines (thorns in Israel's side) until Great King David's Greater Son returns and smites the kingdoms of this world. **Daniel 2:44 The Divine Kingdom**

⁴⁴In the days of those kings the God of heaven will set up a kingdom which will never be destroyed, and *that* kingdom will not be left for another people; it will crush and put an end to all these kingdoms, but it will itself endure forever.

The name Palestine is derived from Philistia. Joel 3:4-5 is also a pertinent passage of prophecy: **Joel 3:4-5**

⁴Moreover, what are you to Me, O Tyre, Sidon and all the regions of Philistia? Are you rendering Me a recompense? But if you do recompense Me, swiftly and speedily I will return your recompense on your head. ⁵Since you have taken My silver and My gold, brought My precious treasures to your temples,

This is a reference to Gentile powers united against the God of Israel. "All the coasts of Philistia," or the Palestinians, seek a recompense—containing the idea of revenge. Why? Although Scripture does not say specifically what is their beef, we can speculate that it is retaliation for the Jews' Law of Return and for Jewish re-emergence in the Land. Palestinians are angry for disinheritance and because of the Islamic doctrine of hegemony. Islam is convinced it will regain all of the Holy Land.

In Bible days, the Philistines were thorns in Israel's side "designed" to bring the Israelites back to God. But whenever they cried to

God for deliverance, he always sent a deliverer! What should our response be today? As believers, it is our duty to preach the Gospel, to support merciful humanitarian causes of all who are suffering amongst Palestinians and Jews, to fast and pray to hasten the harvest of souls and the return of THE Deliverer (Yeshua).

Obadiah 17,19

[17] "But on Mount Zion there will be those who escape, And it will be holy. And the house of Jacob will possess their possessions.

[19] Then *those of* the Negev will possess the mountain of Esau, And *those of* the Shephelah the Philistine *plain*; Also, possess the territory of Ephraim and the territory of Samaria,

And Benjamin *will possess* Gilead.

When was the koran written?

Did Muhammad write the Quran?

No He Didn't, He Was illiterate So He Could Neither Read Nor Write

did he tell his followers what to write down because he could not read or write.?

Muslims believe that the Quran was orally revealed by allah to the Prophet, Muhammad, through the archangel Jibril, incrementally over a period of some 23 years, beginning on 22 December 609 CE, when Muhammad was 40, and concluding in 632, the year of his death. According to tradition, several of Muhammad's companions served as scribes and recorded the revelations. Shortly after his death, the Quran was compiled by the companions, who had written down or memorized parts of it. That is why there are different versions of the koran that were written.

Can Muslims Be Good Americans ?

The Immigration and Nationality Act passed June 27, 1952 revised the laws relating to immigration, naturalization, and nationality for the United States. That act, which became Public Law 414, established both the law and the intent of Congress regarding the immigration of Aliens to the US and remains in effect today. Among the many issues it covers, one in particular, found in Chapter 2

Section 212, (28), (F) is the prohibition of entry to the US if the Alien belongs to an organization seeking to overthrow the government of the United States by 'force, violence, or other unconstitutional means.' This, by its very definition, rules out Islamic immigration to the United States. Islamic immigration to the US would be prohibited under this law because the Koran, Sharia Law and the Hadith all require complete submission to Islam, which is antithetical to the US government, the Constitution, and to the Republic. All Muslims who attest that the Koran is their life's guiding principal subscribe to submission to Islam and its form of government. Whether Islam is a religion is immaterial because the law states that Aliens who are affiliated with any "organization" that advocates the overthrow of our government are prohibited." The ultimate goal of Islamists is to establish Sharia law over the entire world.

Can a Muslim be a good American?

Theologically—no, because his allegiance is to Allah.

no, because he must submit to the mullahs (spiritual leaders) who teach the annihilation of Israel and the destruction of America, the great Satan. no, because he cannot accept the American Constitution since it is based on Biblical principles and he believes the Bible to be corrupt. no, because when we declare 'one nation under God,' we are referring to the Christian's God and not Allah. They obviously cannot be both 'good' Muslims and good Americans; they cannot and will not integrate into the great melting pot of America.

This makes an interesting point and current world observation. Muslims don't assimilate into other countries and cultures, they take over!

Chapter 14

WHAT HAPPENS
WHEN YOU DIE?

∞

Genesis 2:1-8 Thus the heavens and the earth were completed, and all their hosts. ² By the seventh day God completed His work which He had done, and He rested on the seventh day from all His work which He had done. ³ Then God blessed the seventh day and sanctified it, because in it He rested from all His work which God had created and made.

⁴ This is the account of the heavens and the earth when they were created, in the day that the LORD God made earth and heaven. ⁵ Now no shrub of the field was yet in the earth, and no plant of the field had yet sprouted, for the LORD God had not sent rain upon the earth, and there was no man to cultivate the ground. ⁶ But a mist used to rise from the earth and water the whole surface of the ground. ⁷ Then the **LORD God formed man of dust from the ground, and breathed into his nostrils the breath of life; and man became a living being**. ⁸ The LORD God planted a garden toward the east, in Eden; and there He placed the man whom He had formed.

That verse from Genesis 2:7 says everything–man was formed from dust and God breathed into him the breathe of life. God gave him His spirit.

Job 33:4 "The Spirit of God has made me, And the breath of the Almighty gives me life.

WHAT HAPPENS WHEN YOU DIE?

The answer is right there in the Bible. How does the Bible describe death? The Bible describes death as sleep. One reference of sleep to death is Lazarus.

John 11:11-14 [11] This He said, and after that He said to them, "Our friend Lazarus has fallen asleep; but I go, so that I may awaken him out of sleep." [12] The disciples then said to Him, "Lord, if he has fallen asleep, he will recover." [13] Now Jesus had spoken of his death, but they thought that He was speaking of literal sleep. [14] **So Jesus then said to them plainly, "Lazarus is dead,**

That is why Jesus waited three days to get to Lazarus' tomb. To let people know that Lazarus was dead and sleeping.

More than 50 references of sleep to death.

Ecclesiastes 9:5,6 [5] **For the living know they will die; but the dead do not know anything,** nor have they any longer a reward, for their memory is forgotten. [6] Indeed their love, their hate and their zeal have already perished, and they will no longer have a share in all that is done under the sun.

Psalms 146:4 His spirit departs, he returns to the earth; In that very day his thoughts perish.

Revelation 14:13 [13] **And I heard a voice from heaven, saying, "Write, 'Blessed are the dead who die in the Lord from now on!'" "Yes," says the Spirit, "so that they may rest from their labors, for their deeds follow with them."**

When God created Adam, he breathed life into his nostrils.

Genesis 2:7 [7] Then the LORD God formed man of dust from the ground, and breathed into his nostrils the breath of life; and man became a living being.

Immortal soul

Ezekiel 18:4 Behold, all souls are Mine; the soul of the father as well as the soul of the son is Mine. The soul who sins will die.

In Ezekiel it is plain–the soul who sins will die. This is repeated and very clear in Romans.

Romans–wages of sin is death. separated from Jesus for Life. Meaning if you die in sin, you are separated from Jesus forever!

Romans 6:22,23 [22] But now having been freed from sin and enslaved to God, you derive your benefit, resulting in sanctification, and the outcome, eternal life. [23] **For the wages of sin is death, but the free gift of God is eternal life in Christ Jesus our Lord.**

God is the only immortal one. If man dies in sin–it is too late.

1 Timothy 6:15, 16 ¹⁵ which He will bring about at the proper time—He who is the blessed and only Sovereign, the King of kings and Lord of lords, ¹⁶ who alone possesses immortality and dwells in unapproachable light, whom no man has seen or can see. To Him *be* honor and eternal dominion! Amen.

Where do the dead go when they die?

Job 21:32 "While he is carried to the grave, *Men* will keep watch over *his* tomb.

Can the dead come back?

Job 7:8-10 ⁸ "The eye of him who sees me will behold me no longer; Your eyes *will be* on me, but I will not be. ⁹ "When a cloud vanishes, it is gone, So he who goes down to Sheol does not come up.

¹⁰ "He will not return again to his house, nor will his place know him anymore.

David was buried and he sleeps.

Acts 2:29, 34

²⁹ **"Brethren, I may confidently say to you regarding the patriarch David that he both died and was buried, and his tomb is with us to this day.**

³⁴ **For it was not David who ascended into heaven, but he himself says:**

'THE LORD SAID TO MY LORD,

"SIT AT MY RIGHT HAND,

1 Corinthians 15:51-55 [51] Behold, I tell you a mystery; we will not all sleep, but we will all be changed, [52] in a moment, in the twinkling of an eye, at the last trumpet; for the trumpet will sound, and the dead will be raised imperishable, and we will be changed. [53] For this perishable must put on the imperishable, and this mortal must put on immortality. [54] But when this perishable will have put on the imperishable, and this mortal will have put on immortality, then will come about the saying that is written, "DEATH IS SWALLOWED UP in victory. [55] O DEATH, WHERE IS YOUR VICTORY? O DEATH, WHERE IS YOUR STING?"

When you die you sleep is explained and pointed out in 1 Thessalonians 4:13-18

1 Thessalonians 4:13-18 Those Who Died in Christ

[13] But **we do not want you to be uninformed, brethren, about those who are asleep**, so that you will not grieve as do the rest who have no hope. [14] For if we believe that Jesus died and rose again, even so **God will bring with Him those who have fallen asleep in Jesus.** [15] For this we say to you by the word of the Lord, that **we who are alive and remain until the coming of the Lord, will not precede those who have fallen asleep.** [16] For the Lord Himself will descend from heaven with a shout, with the voice of *the* archangel and with the trumpet of God, and the dead in Christ will rise first. [17] Then we who are alive and remain will be caught up together with them in the clouds to meet the Lord in the air, and so we shall always be with the Lord. [18] Therefore comfort one another with these words.

Put very plainly, If you go to heaven when you die, where do all those who are asleep in Christ come from?

There is it very plain. When you die, you do not go to heaven. You sleep until Jesus comes back in the clouds. When Jesus comes in the clouds, the dead in Christ rise to meet him and those that are alive in Christ meet them in the air.

These are words of encouragement. I would hate that my loved ones were in heaven and watching me. I prefer that they are asleep and If I am alive, I will meet them in the air. It is also very comforting to know that when I die, I will sleep and when I wake I will be with the Lord. A story about a student and a Rabbi. The student asked the Rabbi, "how do I get to Heaven?" The Rabbi told him that he had to be saved. The student asked "how do I get saved?" The Rabbi replied "ask for forgiveness". The student asked "when do I need to ask for forgiveness?" The Rabbi said "the day before you die"

remember the story of the thief on the cross.

Luke 23:42,43 [42] And he was saying, "Jesus, remember me when You come in Your kingdom!" [43] And He said to him, "Truly I say to you today, you shall be with Me in Paradise."

Jesus was telling the criminal on the cross today (on that day) that he would be with Christ when he returns.

John 20:16,17 [16] Jesus *said to her, "Mary!" She turned and *said to Him in Hebrew, "Rabboni!" (which means, Teacher). [17] Jesus *said to her, "Stop clinging to Me, for I have not yet ascended to the Father; but go to My brethren and say to them, 'I ascend to My Father and your Father, and My God and your God.'"

To be absent from the body is to be present in the Lord

2 Cor 5:8 [8] we are of good courage, I say, and prefer rather to be absent from the body and to be at home with the Lord.

When is the second coming?

1 Cor 15:51-53 [51] Behold, I tell you a mystery; we will not all sleep, but we will all be changed, [52] in a moment, in the twinkling of an eye, at the last trumpet; for the trumpet will sound, and the dead will be raised imperishable, and we will be changed. [53] For this perishable must put on the imperishable, and this mortal must put on immortality.

2Tim 4:7 [7] I have fought the good fight, I have finished the course, I have kept the faith;

1 John 5:11-13 [11] And the testimony is this, that God has given us eternal life, and this life is in His Son. [12] He who has the Son has the life; he who does not have the Son of God does not have the life. [13] These things I have written to you who believe in the name of the Son of God, so that you may know that you have eternal life.

Remember **Genesis 2:7 Then the Lᴏʀᴅ God formed man of dust from the ground, and breathed into his nostrils the breath of life; and man became a living being.**

The term 'Ashes to ashes' comes from a burial service.. The text of that service is adapted from the Biblical text, **Genesis 3:19 (King James Version):** In the sweat of thy face shalt thou eat bread, till thou return unto the ground; for out of it wast thou taken: for dust thou art, and unto dust shalt thou return.

When we die our soul returns to God until Jesus comes in the air. The dead in Christ rise to meet him and those alive in Christ meet them in the air.

Remember **Romans 6:23–²³ For the wages of sin is death, but the free gift of God is eternal life in Christ Jesus our Lord.**

If you die in sin...it is too late. You should, sincerely, ask now for forgiveness and live daily with the Lord.

It is very reassuring that when you die you sleep. You do not go to heaven immediately, but you sleep until Christ's return. I would hate to think that my parents have been in heaven looking down and seeing some of the stuff that I did in my early years. I much prefer to know that they are asleep and I will meet them in the air when Jesus comes.

The only thing that we need to do to assure that we meet Jesus in the clouds is to not die in sin. So, stay in communication with the Holy Spirit, Pray often, and should you sin, sincerely ask for forgiveness,.

9 781545 674048